CULTURES OF THE WORLD®

BULGARIA

Kirilka Stavreva & Lynette Quek

Marshall Cavendish
Benchmark

New York

PICTURE CREDITS
Cover photo: © Hideo Haga/HAGA/The Image Works
alt.TYPE/Reuters: 18, 27, 33, 38, 41, 56, 124 • Audrius Tomonis: 135 • Bes Stock/alamy: 9, 21, 22, 48, 50, 53, 55, 64, 76, 77, 86, 94, 116, 117, 122 • Björn Klingwall: 11, 37, 40, 42, 43, 71, 80, 102, 109, 129 • Hutchison: 10, 34, 39, 58, 59, 69, 70, 72, 74, 75, 85, 92, 101, 111, 120, 121, 123, 125 • Jude Fredricsen: 32, 88, 90 • Keystone Press: 19 • Marie-Claire Seeley: 60, 63, 82, 84, 106, 110 • Marka: 46, 47 • National Geographic: 36 • Per Sandvik: 126 • R Ian Llyod/age footstock: 1, 6, 7, 44, 52, 95, 100, 104 • Ro Herzog: 4, 12, 14, 17, 20, 31, 62, 78, 79, 93, 97, 105, 107, 108, 113, 118 • Photolibrary: 16, 25, 54, 66, 98, 130 • Stockfood: 131 • Superstock: 5, 30, 114 • Susan Hawkins: 23, 28 • Susanna Burton: 8, 65, 67, 68, 73, 83, 96, 103 • Tan Chung Lee: 3, 13, 15, 91, 119, 127

PRECEDING PAGE
Smiling Bulgarian girls in traditional costume at the annual Roses Festival.

Publisher (U.S.): Michelle Bisson
Editors: Deborah Grahame, Mabelle Yeo, Crystal Ouyang
Copyreader: Daphne Hougham
Designers: Jailani Basari, Sean Lee, Benson Tan
Cover picture researcher: Connie Gardner
Picture researchers: Thomas Khoo, Joshua Ang

Marshall Cavendish Benchmark
99 White Plains Road
Tarrytown, NY 10591
Web site: www.marshallcavendish.us

Originated and designed by Times Editions Private Limited
An imprint of Marshall Cavendish International (Asia) Private Limited
A member of Times Publishing Limited

All Internet sites were correct and accurate at the time of printing. All monetary figures in this publication are in U.S. dollars.

Library of Congress Cataloging-in-Publication Data
Stavreva, Kirilka.
  Bulgaria / by Kirilka Stavreva & Lynette Quek. — 2nd ed.
    p. cm. — (Cultures of the world)
  Summary: "Provides comprehensive information on the geography, history, wildlife, governmental structure, economy, cultural
    diversity, peoples, religion, and culture of Bulgaria"— Provided by publisher.
  Includes bibliographical references and index.
    ISBN 978-0-7614-2078-1
  1. Bulgaria—Juvenile literature. I. Quek, Lynette. II. Title. III. Series.
  DR55.S76 2007
  949.9—dc22   2006101730

Printed in China

9 8 7 6 5 4 3 2 1

CONTENTS

A Bulgarian mother and child.

Winter in Plovdiv.

INTRODUCTION

BULGARIA IS A COUNTRY that is little known to the world. There is much more to Bulgaria than its stolid Communist past. Its cities and towns are a charming mix of ancient and modern, boasting layer upon layer of a rich, storied heritage.

It is a stronghold of Slavic traditions and language, where elements of a deeply rooted folk culture are preserved. It is also a land of mythical beauty, with a long and dramatic history. Its people are resilient and courageous, rising above a succession of repressive empires, including the Roman, Byzantine, and Ottoman.

The influence of multiple cultures can be tasted in Bulgarian cuisine, heard in its music, and seen in its ancient ruins and architecture. This blend of the very oldest with the very newest epitomizes Bulgaria today. Receiving its membership in the European Union in 2007, this old Balkan country is just beginning a renaissance, while wearing its history on its sleeve.

GEOGRAPHY

BULGARIA SITS IN THE HEART of the Balkan Peninsula, in southeastern Europe. The country has an eastern coast washed by the Black Sea, giving it strategic access to both the Sea of Marmara and the Mediterranean Sea. Turkey is its southeastern neighbor and Greece its southwestern.

To the west lie Macedonia and Serbia. In the north the Danube River separates it from Romania. The total area of Bulgaria is 42,823 square miles (110,912 square km), making it only slightly larger than the state of Tennessee in the United States.

For such a small country, Bulgaria's natural terrain is strikingly varied. There are majestic mountains cut by deep gorges, fertile plains and lowlands, and a dramatic seacoast. No single feature dominates the landscape, which may change with every bend of the road.

The Balkan range of mountains divides the country into the two parts of north and south, with the Black Sea coast forming a third region.

Above: **The Bulgarian Black Sea coast has long sandy beaches alternating with steep cliffs.**

Opposite: **The pristine slopes of Pirin National Park attract hikers from all over Europe.**

A PARADISE ON EARTH

How Bulgaria became a land of such variety and beauty is explained in an old legend. It seems that on the day that God was giving out land to the various nations, he parceled it all out and forgot the Bulgarians.

When a Bulgarian man complained, God thought for a moment, and then smiled broadly, "I have the solution for you. Since all the world has been already divided up, I will give your people a piece of paradise."

THREE DISTINCT REGIONS

The Balkan range divides the country into two parts. The fertile Danubian plain is in the north, and in the south lies a region of high mountains, enclosed valleys, and the large Thracian plain. The third distinct area is the Black Sea coast.

Northern Bulgaria has been the country's golden granary since the seventh century, when the Slav and Bulgar tribes united, forming the beginning of Bulgaria. In recent times, a prosperous food and beverage industry has developed in the region, based on the production of grains and oilseeds.

Sunflowers flourish in northern Bulgaria, an area rich in the production of grains and oilseeds.

Veliko Turnovo, Turnovo (also Tarnovo) for short, is one of Bulgaria's oldest cities and overlooks the winding Yantra River. Its stone fortress walls testify to its importance as the medieval capital. But in modern-day Turnovo, heavy industry is very significant, along with historical monuments such as churches and castles.

In southern Bulgaria warm Mediterranean air reaches the region along the river valleys, and the Balkan range acts as a climatic barrier against cold northern influences. These weather conditions, along with fertile soils and abundant mountain waters, favor the growing of vegetables, fruits, including grapes, and cotton. The Bulgarian oil-bearing rose also thrives there.

Most of the big cities in southern Bulgaria, including the capital, Sofia, are encircled by prosperous farms. Light industry, including tobacco processing and textiles, is well represented in this region. So is heavy industry, such as nonferrous metallurgy, machine making, chemicals manufacturing, timber processing, and cement production.

The highest mountains in the Balkan Peninsula rise in the southwest of Bulgaria. The rugged profiles of the Rila and Pirin ranges attract hikers and skiers from all over Europe, and the gently rolling slopes of the Rhodope range provide excellent conditions for winter tourism. Vast mountain pastures enable cattle breeding and the raising of sheep.

The eastern parts of the Rhodope are inhabited mainly by Bulgarian Turks, who make good use of the favorable soils and the sunny, arid climate to cultivate top-grade Oriental tobacco.

The mountains and scenic lakes in the Rhodope region are popular with tourists.

THE HOMELAND OF YOGURT

Yogurt is a staple of the Bulgarian diet. It can be eaten plain or made into a drink, salad dressing, or cold soup. Bulgarian yogurt is usually made from cow's milk, but sheep's or goat's milk are also used. Yogurt from sheep's milk is considered a delicacy.

The bacteria responsible for the fermentation of Bulgarian yogurt thrives best only within the country. Bulgarians believe that, apart from being a rich source of calcium, their yogurt also contributes to their longevity.

BLACK SEA COAST

The country's eastern coastline is approximately 219 miles (352 km) long. This is the Black Sea coast, where steep cliffs with underwater caves alternate with long sandy beaches and junglelike vegetation grows around the mouths of rivers. Small picturesque fishing towns lie side by side with large industrial port cities. The petrochemical, shipbuilding, metal processing, and electrical appliance industries are well developed in this region. The raw materials are imported, and finished products are exported to numerous other countries.

Cheese and yogurt are produced from sheep raised on mountain pastures in southern Bulgaria.

FOUR SEASONS

Bulgaria has a temperate continental climate. The weather is conditioned, however, by diverse elements such as the humid cyclones of the North Atlantic, the severe anticyclones of the Siberian plain, and mild air currents that waft in from the Mediterranean Sea.

The average annual temperatures are about 51°F (11°C) for northern Bulgaria and 56°F (13°C) for southern Bulgaria. The coldest winter month is January, when temperatures average 23°F (–5°C) in the north and up to 36°F (2°C) in the south.

It is much colder in the mountains, while winters at the Black Sea coast are milder, with temperatures averaging around 36°F (2°C).

Summers are hot but tolerable. July is the hottest month for the whole country, with temperatures hovering between 70 and 75°F (21 and 24°C), although it is cooler in the high mountains.

Rain is the most common precipitation, but there are heavy winter snowfalls across the northern plains and in the mountains. Precipitation is evenly distributed across the country and throughout the four seasons.

Because of the diverse terrain, there are no tornadoes, hurricanes, sandstorms, or other strong winds of that nature. The only constant air currents are the fresh breezes along the seacoast.

A village in the mountains can be very cold in winter.

RIVERS, LAKES, AND SPRINGS

Bulgaria has over 526 rivers, though the only navigable river is the Danube at 300 miles (483 km) long. Other major rivers include the Iskur, which flows northward from the Rila and through Sofia before joining the Danube, and the Maritsa, which defines the border between neighboring Greece and Turkey.

There are about 330 lakes in Bulgaria; the largest are the Black Sea lakes, believed to have medicinal qualities. Sreburna Lake near the Danube is the habitat of rare birds such as the pink pelican and the wild swan. The high-mountain glacial lakes in the Rila and Pirin mountain ranges are popular attractions.

Many natural mineral springs and baths are found all over the country. Bulgaria has some 500 deposits of mineral waters from over 1,600 sources.

FLORA AND FAUNA

Bulgaria is a paradise for botanists and nature lovers. It is home to more than 3,750 vascular plant species and 13,000 animal species. It has over 250 native plants, such as the Rila cowslip and Pirin poppy, and the Bulgarian oil-bearing rose is the only descendant of the Persian rose surviving in Europe. The country ranks fifth in Europe for its plant diversity.

Plant relics of bygone geological eras are also to be found. These include the Strandja periwinkle, white and black spruce, sycamore, and the near-extinct edelweiss. Deciduous oak, elm, and beech, together with coniferous pine, fir, and spruce, are the dominant varieties of trees. The woods are the habitat of wild animals such as bears, wolves, and red deer. Bulgaria supports three national parks, 10 nature parks, and 90 wildlife reserves, with 389 protected plant species and 473 protected animal species.

Despite its small territory, Bulgaria is extremely rich in endemic, or native, plants. It is also home to 750 types of medicinal plants and is the biggest exporter of such plants in Europe.

Oil-bearing roses thrive in the fertile soils of southern Bulgaria.

The small town of Melnik, hardly bigger than a village, tucked against the Pirin Mountains.

TOWN AND COUNTRY

Most Bulgarians live either in industrialized cities or in villages with an agrarian economic base. This system of settlement has evolved from centuries of development, largely influenced by the variety of geographic conditions. There is little difference between the lifestyle of villagers and that of city dwellers.

Bulgarian villages, sprinkled all over the country, are older and far more numerous than the cities. The biggest and most prosperous villages are concentrated in the fertile plains of northern and southern Bulgaria. Mountain villages tend to be smaller, poorer, and clustered closer to one another. Their populations have dwindled substantially, because young people have migrated to the cities in search of employment and cultural diversity. During the 19th century urbanization became especially marked. The process accelerated during the socialist period, when the country developed an industrial base.

SOFIA Bulgaria's bustling capital lies at the foot of Mount Vitosha and has a population of 1.22 million. It was built on the site of an ancient Roman fortress, remains of which can still be seen in the underpasses in the city center. Architecturally, Sofia is a mix of early 20th-century Baroque buildings, Byzantine-style churches, a sprinkling of mosques and Turkish baths, massive concrete socialist structures dating from the 1950s, and modern glass buildings popular during the 1990s.

Sofia became the capital in 1879 after Bulgaria gained independence from the Turkish Ottoman Empire. At the time, the young capital was no bigger than a village. Today, however, it is the country's largest city and its political, cultural, and commercial center.

PLOVDIV Founded in 432 B.C., the country's second-largest city lies on both sides of the Maritsa River in the middle of the Thracian Plain. It is one of Europe's oldest cities and has a population of 341,500. Cobblestone streets twist up the hillsides of the Old Town, crowded with ancient ruins and buildings from the 18th and 19th centuries, built in typical National Revival style.

VARNA This is Bulgaria's third largest city, with a population of 312,000, and its second-biggest port, after Burgas. Known to the ancient Greeks as Odessus, Varna is now an important industrial, transportation, and cultural center. Several luxury resorts line the beaches adjacent to the city. In the summer hordes of tourists from all over the world flock to these resorts for a taste of what the "Summer Capital" has to offer.

A street scene in the capital city of Sofia.

HISTORY

THE MASS MIGRATIONS OF THE Slavs to the Balkan Peninsula during the sixth and seventh centuries spearheaded the founding of the Bulgarian state. Before that, ancient Thracian, Greek, Roman, and Byzantine civilizations had set their marks on the country's cultural heritage.

The name Bulgaria is not Slavic, but derived from the nomadic tribe of Bulgars that came from the vast treeless steppes north of the Black Sea. The Bulgars were warriors, disciplined and obedient to their chief, Khan Asparuh, who led them in seizing Slavic lands in Moesia and Little Scythia on the northeast fringe of Byzantium. The mighty Byzantine Empire was compelled to recognize the authority of the Bulgars in the lands they had captured.

Above: **Thracian ruins, uncovered by archaeologists in the city of Plovdiv.**

Opposite: **A spectacular corridor in Rila Monastery, one of the oldest buildings in southern Bulgaria.**

FIRST FOR THE SLAVS

In the year A.D. 681 a treaty was signed in which the Byzantine rulers agreed to pay tribute to the newly founded state of Slavs and Bulgars, known as the First Bulgarian Kingdom. This was a precedent and an achievement for the seven Slavic tribes, made possible by their vigorous alliance with the Bulgars.

Because Bulgaria then controlled major roads linking Eastern Europe and Asia with the interior of the European continent, it became the focal point of strife and confrontation between East and West in medieval Europe. Bulgaria's first decades were marked by a life-and-death struggle for survival against the Byzantine Empire, and this great common effort gave the multiethnic tribes a sense of unity. The country became a barrier against nomadic incursions from the northeast. Bulgaria thus contributed greatly to political stability in this part of Europe.

Statues of Saints Cyril and Methodius, in front of the National Library in Sofia.

CLASSICAL HERITAGE

The civic peace of the country was protected by a severe legal code introduced by Khan Krum, remembered in history as Krum the Terrible. According to his laws, defamation was punishable by death, robbery by breaking the anklebones, and denying alms to a beggar by the seizure of property in the name of the ruler.

The amalgamation of the Slavs and Bulgars was finally accomplished with the adoption of Orthodox Christianity by Boris I in the ninth century. This memorable event came after long negotiations with the Church of Rome and the Church in Constantinople, enabling the Bulgarian Church to win a marked degree of independence.

The link with Constantinople in terms of religion and politics gave the Bulgarians a classical heritage, a religious structure, Byzantine political and legal concepts, as well as the best-defined national culture in all of Europe at that period.

The leaders of the Bulgarian state were well aware that the Christianization of the country could lead to a Byzantine cultural conquest of Bulgaria. That is why Prince Boris eagerly adopted the Slavic alphabet created by the Greek missionary brothers Cyril and Methodius, and worked out a plan for spreading the church liturgy and learning—not in Greek, but in the spoken Slavic language and the new Cyrillic lettering of his country.

Thus the Bulgarian national identity was forged—through the new state religion, the growth of education and its spread to widening circles, and through the development of a Bulgarian literary language.

The First Bulgarian Kingdom reached the zenith of its political, military, social, and cultural development during the reign of Czar Simeon (889–927), known as the Bulgarian Charlemagne. He made a determined effort to oust the Byzantine Empire from the Balkan Peninsula and to gain recognition for himself as an emperor in the medieval family of Christian monarchs.

GOLDEN AGE OF CULTURE

This period was marked by a surge toward political and religious equality with Byzantium, the territorial expansion of Bulgaria over the greater part of the Balkans, and by a flowering of Bulgarian culture.

The new capital city of Preslav was renowned for its magnificent architecture. Along with Ohrid at the opposite end of Czar Simeon's empire, Preslav emerged as a leading center of Slavic literature and culture.

Bishop Clement of Ohrid and his students encouraged an enlightened approach to cultural development. Writers of the period were intensely conscious of their role as champions of the new Slavic culture. Having incorporated much from Byzantine culture, Bulgaria in turn influenced the Serbs, Russians, and Romanians.

Crown Prince Boris (1894–1943) came to the throne as Boris III. His son succeeded him as Simeon II, but the Bulgarian monarchy was abolished in 1946.

The distinctive stone walls of Veliko Turnovo, which reached its glory in the 13th century as the capital and fortress of the Second Bulgarian Kingdom.

SURVIVAL AND TRIUMPH

After Czar Simeon's death, the Bulgarian kingdom plunged into a deep social and political crisis and eventually fell to Byzantium. The eastern Bulgarian provinces and the capital, Preslav, were taken in A.D. 971. The southeastern provinces, with Ohrid as the new state capital, were for a long time successful in staving off defeat, but in 1018 they were finally conquered by the Byzantine emperor Basil II, who was nicknamed the Bulgar Slayer.

For over a century and a half of Byzantine colonization, the Bulgarian people suffered excessive taxation, systematic destruction of their literature and their cultural monuments, and other forms of abuse. Yet throughout those years they kept alive a spirit of freedom and resistance. One after another, uprisings and rebellions against the Byzantine rulers shook the foundations of the empire. The armed resistance of the Bulgarian feudal lords was backed by the vast Bogomil movement—a religious and social organization whose ideology embodied strongly felt anti-Byzantine trends.

In 1185 the aristocratic *bolyar* (or boyar) brothers Ivan and Petar Asen led a movement to free Bulgarians in the lands between the Danube River and the Balkan Mountains. This led to the establishment of the Second Bulgarian Kingdom, with the Balkan fortress of Veliko Turnovo as the capital. Kaloyan, who succeeded the Asen brothers, completed the liberation of the Bulgarian population of Thrace, the Rhodope region, and Macedonia. His diplomacy led to the recognition of the kingdom by Byzantium and papal Rome.

The restored kingdom's hour of triumph came during the reign of Ivan Asen II (1218–41). His skillful diplomatic maneuvers expanded Bulgaria's territory. Once again it stretched "from sea to shining sea," from the Black Sea to the Adriatic, as it had during Czar Simeon's Golden Age.

Another view of Veliko Turnovo. In its heyday, it was a city of economic and cultural supremacy.

A SECOND ROME

Veliko Turnovo was extolled as the city "saved by God" and called "a second Rome" and "a new Constantinople." The vast Bulgarian state saw a new cultural and economic upsurge. It extended its political and trade relations with a number of European states. There was an enormous surge in the construction of churches, fortresses, and bridges. Aristocratic patronage of trades and the arts flourished as never before.

By the second half of the 13th century, nevertheless, Bulgaria faced another grave political crisis. A peasant revolt and fierce attacks from Mongol tribes had weakened it, making it easy prey for the new great power that was rising in the east of Europe—the Ottoman Empire.

The Czar Liberator Monument in Sofia.

STRUGGLE FOR THE NATION

In the last half of the 14th century, the Ottoman Empire conquered the Bulgarian people and their divided rulers. The development of the independent Bulgarian state was to be interrupted for nearly five centuries more. Hundreds of settlements, fortresses, churches, and monasteries were reduced to ashes by the Ottoman invaders. The political and spiritual elite of the Bulgarian people was exiled or exterminated, and the clergy was dispersed or ruthlessly repressed. The national Bulgarian church was subordinated to Constantinople. Bulgarians were excluded from local administration, and all of the country's resources were put at the disposal of the Ottoman war machine.

The conquest was marked by a massive slaughter of soldiers and civilians. Tens of thousands of Bulgarians were sold in the slave markets; thousands more sought refuge abroad; Christians were forced en masse to convert to Islam, or were forced to move to the Asian parts of the Ottoman Empire.

To some extent this fanatic persecution of the Bulgarian "infidels" roused the national and religious feelings of the Bulgarian people, compelling them to define their national identity and to preserve their cultural traditions and values. This they succeeded in doing, against great odds. From the peasants in secluded mountain villages to the monks in the few surviving monasteries, all made their contributions. So too did the *haidouks* (hai-DOOKS), members of the spontaneous underground movement against Turkish domination.

By the 18th century the spirit of the people was truly stirred—by the economic upsurge of the Bulgarian community within the Ottoman Empire, by its commercial contacts with people from near and distant lands, and by the influence of the European Enlightenment movement that rejected many traditional ideas.

The first to spur the people on was Father Paisiy Hilendarski from the Chilendar monastery on Mount Athos in Greece. In 1762 the monk completed his *Slav-Bulgarian History*, an ardent nationalistic appeal to the Bulgarian people to cherish their language and culture, to take pride in their glorious historical past, and to fight on for their liberation from the oppressive Ottomans.

NATIONAL REVIVAL MOVEMENT

In the first half of the 19th century, the momentum for a National Revival gathered pace. Schools and library clubs began to open in the towns and villages. This gave an impetus to literature and journalism. Church and urban architecture also flourished, along with the visual arts.

In 1870 the Ottoman government finally gave in to the long and determined struggle of the Bulgarians for a national church separate from the Greek Patriarchate. The independent Church of the Bulgarian Exarchate became the first national political institution, one that was recognized by Turkey.

Elegant cloisters of a town museum.

LEVSKI: APOSTLE OF FREEDOM

The purest figure of the liberation movement was Vassil Levski (1837–73), called the Apostle of Freedom by peasants and scholars alike. Levski was a saint of the revolution. Guided by an unflinching confidence in the Bulgarian national spirit, he decided his country could be liberated only with the participation of the entire population. Thus he devoted his boundless energy and organizational talent to underground work in towns and villages throughout Bulgaria.

Apart from setting up local revolutionary committees, Levski drew up the statutes of the organization. Here is how he envisioned the democratic future of his beloved country:

"In our Bulgaria things will be different from how they are in Turkey now. All the nationalities in our country, Turks, Jews, and others, will live under the same pure and sacred laws.

"There will be no king in Bulgaria, but 'popular rule' and to each 'his due.' . . . A free and pure republic.

"We yearn to see our fatherland free, and when that day comes I will be content just to keep watch over the ducks at pasture."

Betrayed by a fellow Bulgarian and captured by the Turks, Levski was hanged outside Sofia on February 19, 1873. To this day Bulgarians commemorate his life and death by laying flowers on the modest monument that marks the place of his execution.

APRIL UPRISING

Nationalistic fervor led to an armed revolutionary campaign. This movement of National Revival aimed at liberating Bulgaria from Ottoman domination and culminated in the April Uprising of 1876, which was suppressed with unprecedented cruelty and revenge. The Ottoman army and insurgent bands slaughtered men, women, and children. Some 80 Bulgarian villages were incinerated and their inhabitants massacred.

On their way to the gallows, the organizers of the National Revival revolt rejoiced that their goal had been achieved and expressed their faith in Slavic solidarity. One of them, the military commander Georgi Benkovski rejoiced, exclaiming, "Such a mortal wound have I inflicted to the heart of the tyrant that he will never recover from it. As for Russia—she is now welcome!"

In 1877 Russia did declare war on the Ottoman Empire, and thousands of Bulgarians volunteered their services. Finally, on March 3, 1878, Turkey signed a treaty of capitulation, the San Stefano peace settlement, recognizing Bulgaria's independence.

STRUGGLE FOR UNIFICATION

The San Stefano settlement ensured the political liberation of the Bulgarians in Moesia (between the Danube River and the Balkan Mountains), northern Thrace, and Macedonia. Under the sovereignty of its very own church and state, the Bulgarian nation felt free, united, and poised for a great future ahead.

But the dream was shattered a short five months later by the Berlin Congress of the European superpowers. To satisfy the claims of England and Austria, the Bulgarian state had three of its main provinces snatched away, with only Moesia and the region around Sofia retaining their status.

ISSUE OVER MACEDONIA

Thrace, under the name of Eastern Rumelia, was returned to the Ottoman Empire. Macedonia and the Aegean coast were also returned to the Ottomans, without any undertaking to protect the Bulgarian population. The decisions of the Berlin Congress thwarted aspirations for national unity and hindered Bulgaria's political, economic, and cultural development for a long time. The decisions also planted the explosive "Macedonian Question" in European politics.

Bulgaria did not resign itself to the slicing up of its nation. The Eastern Rumelia province proclaimed its alliance with the principality of Bulgaria in 1885, and the population of southern Thrace and Macedonia struggled determinedly for their liberty, but to no avail.

The Veltchova Zavera war monument in Veliko Turnovo.

THE MACEDONIAN QUESTION

The ethnic identity of the Macedonians has long been a controversial issue. Until the 19th century "Macedonia" usually indicated a geographical area populated mainly by Bulgarians, with a mix of Greeks, Turks, Albanians, Gypsies, Armenians, Jews, and, marginally, Serbs.

Many prominent figures of the National Revival were born in Macedonia but always referred to themselves as Bulgarian. When the Berlin Congress of 1878 restored Macedonia to the Ottoman Empire, its population loudly protested the separation from their conationals. After the Balkan Wars in the first two decades of the 20th century, Macedonia was divided among Greece, Serbia, and Bulgaria. Forced population transfers followed, largely removing Slavic speakers from Greek Macedonia and Greek speakers from the rest of the territory. Today, over a quarter of Bulgarians can trace their roots to Macedonia.

The notion of a distinct Macedonian nationality, with its own language and history, was introduced in the 20th century by President Josip Tito's regime in the former Yugoslavia, with Joseph Stalin's approval. When the Yugoslav Federation broke up, the independent state of Macedonia was created in 1991. Bulgaria was the first country to give full recognition to the new state of Macedonia, despite vehement Greek protests. All the same, the Bulgarian people have been reluctant to acknowledge the existence of a Macedonian nationality or to recognize the Macedonian language.

Bulgaria became a Communist state after 1944 and began to echo the Soviet Union in many spheres. But in some areas, such as central control of the arts, it proved less restrictive than the former Soviet Union.

THE BALKAN WARS

Until World War II, Bulgaria pursued the dream of restoring the lands of the San Stefano Treaty, engaging in a series of ill-fated Balkan wars. After repelling a Serbian invasion only weeks after the unification of 1885, the fledgling Bulgarian state formed a new alliance with Greece, Serbia, and Montenegro.

In the First Balkan War in 1912, the coalition forced Turkey to give up its remaining Balkan territories, but extremist nationalistic fervor split up the new alliance. This consequently led to the Second Balkan War in 1913, fought by Bulgaria, Romania, Serbia, Greece, and Turkey. It ended in a national catastrophe for Bulgaria, as territory was lost.

World War I tore away even more lands from the country and ruined its industry and agriculture, all of which resulted in a severe political crisis. Crushed and humiliated, Bulgaria completely lost faith in her nationalistic ideals.

IN THE SOVIET BLOC

During World War II, Bulgaria was a reluctant ally of Germany. It declared a symbolic war on Great Britain and the United States, but its government did not send troops into combat and declined to deport Bulgarian Jews to the death camps of Poland.

In September 1944, while the Bulgarian government was conducting peace talks with the Allies, the Soviet Union declared war on Bulgaria. In conjunction with the Soviet offensive, power in Sofia was seized by a Communist-led coalition called the Fatherland Front.

The stage was thus set for the communization of the country—a process that was completed two years later—despite resistance from democratic forces. Bulgaria then became known as the Soviet Union's most faithful ally, copying the twists and turns of Soviet policies. With the Communist Party in charge, pervasive state ownership became the order of the day, and all aspects of the economy fell under state control.

Nevertheless, the Bulgarian model was in some ways significantly different from the Soviet system. For example, it paid more careful attention to agriculture, raising the rural population's living standards, and the country's achievements in foreign trade were fairly impressive.

This monument to Lenin in Sofia was pulled down during Bulgaria's "gentle revolution."

THORNY PATH TO DEMOCRACY

Bulgaria's "gentle revolution" began with the forced resignation of the dictator Todor Zhivkov in November 1989. Zhivkov's fall set off a wave of rallies. Tens of thousands of demonstrators converged on the central squares of the capital and the big cities, demanding free elections and the end of the regime.

To the credit of those involved—the reforming wing of the Communist Party, which took over from Zhivkov's old guard, and the young alliance of democratic organizations—Bulgaria managed to break away from Communist rule without bloodshed and violence.

Lengthy negotiations went on between the reforming Communist Party, renamed the Bulgarian Socialist Party (BSP), and the Union of Democratic Forces (UDF). The talks led to an agreement on how elections for a Grand

A peaceful group at one of the major demonstrations held in the country after 1989.

National Assembly were to be held. The assembly's task was to work out a new democratic constitution, and that was accomplished in 1991.

After the initial political elation over the first taste of freedom, the country was confronted with a far more daunting prospect. The wounds of a nation divided over its Communist past had to be healed, the economy was in tatters and needed mending, and the country had to be made a hospitable part of the new unified Europe.

PRESENT-DAY BULGARIA

In 1990 Bulgaria had its first taste of democracy when Zhelyu Zhelev of UDF became its first postwar noncommunist president, from 1990 to 1997. The 1990s were marked by constant public unrest, political instability, and economic crises, as the republic embarked on its transition into a free-market economy after the collapse of the Soviet system.

In 2001 the abolished Bulgarian monarchy made a dramatic comeback when the former king, Simeon Saxe-Coburg-Gotha, was elected prime minister, a position he retained until 2005. Rapid inflation, high unemployment, and continued economic uncertainty caused widespread disillusionment in the early 2000s.

Under Simeon, the country pressed ahead with reforms and eventually achieved growth. Unemployment fell from the high of 20 percent, inflation came under control, and foreign relations improved. In 2006 progress continued under the stewardship of Bulgaria's new prime minister, Sergei Stanishev, and president, Georgi Purvanov.

In 2004 Bulgaria officially became a member of the North Atlantic Treaty Organization (NATO), and it joined the European Union (EU) in 2007. The prospect of EU membership had, in the years leading to integration into the EU, stimulated a variety of market reforms designed to meet EU economic standards and entry requirements.

The summer of 1990 was an uneasy time for Bulgarian politicians in power, as ordinary people, students, and the country's intellectuals poured out in thousands demanding better mandates for their nation.

HISTORY OF THE BULGARIAN COMMUNIST PARTY

For 45 years the Bulgarian Communist Party (BCP) had a constitutionally guaranteed right to authority in the country. It commanded all aspects of social, economic, cultural, and educational life. Membership in the party was high compared with ruling Communist parties in other countries. As a political power, it had a long and tumultuous history.

Founded as a workers' social-democratic party in 1891, it was renamed the Bulgarian Communist Party in 1919. Its Communist symbols were even incorporated into the state coat of arms (*right*). It became a cofounder and an active member of the Third Communist International. After the seizure of power by the military-royalist coalition in 1923, the leadership of the BCP fled to Moscow. Until World War II the party led a double life as an underground political force within the country, while its surviving leaders were sheltered abroad.

During World War II the underground BCP committed acts of sabotage and assassinated police officials and fascist functionaries, but did not organize a general insurrection. The BCP's road to power began with two concurrent events: Soviet troops crossed into Bulgaria in September 1944 and Sofia was seized by the leftist political alliance of the Fatherland Front.

Once in power the BCP mobilized the army and the economy for the battle against Germany, purged the Fatherland Front coalition of its competitors, and earned Soviet respect as an effective and loyal ally. From this point on, until the emergence of democracy in 1989, the history of the BCP closely followed that of Soviet political life, and its political grip remained firm and virtually uncontested.

BULGARIAN CONSTITUTION

The constitution of the Republic of Bulgaria was ratified on July 12, 1991. After a period of deep instability in the 1990s, governance in Bulgaria was stabilized in 2001 with the election of Simeon Saxe-Coburg-Gotha as prime minister.

EXECUTIVE BRANCH Bulgaria's president, Georgi Purvanov (since 2002), is the chief of state and commander of the armed forces. He is largely a symbolic figure, representing national unity. The president and vice president are elected every five years by direct popular vote and can be reelected once. Bulgaria's prime minister, Sergei Stanishev (since 2005), is the head of government. The prime minister is selected by the president and approved by the National Assembly (parliament). The prime minister nominates the Council of Ministers (cabinet), which must be approved by parliament. The council is responsible for managing the state budget, enforcing state policy, and maintaining law and order.

Bulgaria's parliament building, the National Assembly, in Sofia.

LEGISLATIVE BRANCH The unicameral National Assembly has 240 members, who are elected for four-year terms by direct popular vote. A party must gain at least 4 percent of the popular vote to be represented. The assembly enacts laws, schedules presidential elections, approves prime ministers and cabinet ministers, ratifies international treaties and agreements, and declares war.

JUDICIAL BRANCH The Supreme Administrative Court and Supreme Court of Cassation (meaning annulling or cancelling), the highest courts of appeal, rule in the lower courts. The Supreme Judicial Council oversees the system and appoints judges and prosecutors. Its 25 members serve five-year terms. The Constitutional Court, consisting of 12 judges serving nine-year terms, interprets the constitutionality of laws and treaties. It can repeal laws that it deems unconstitutional.

Two policemen on a street in Sofia.

ADMINISTRATIVE REGIONS

Bulgaria is divided into 28 administrative regions or provinces (*oblasti*), which are subdivided into 262 self-governing municipalities. Sofia and the region surrounding it is a separate jurisdiction, comparable with Washington, D.C.

REGIONAL AND LOCAL GOVERNMENT

Regional governors are selected by the Council of Ministers. Municipalities are run by mayors, who serve four-year terms, and by municipal councils, which are directly elected legislative bodies. Local governments enforce policies at the local level, but their revenues depend on the central government.

POLITICAL PARTIES

The parties that have dominated Bulgarian politics since the 1990s are the Bulgarian Socialist Party (BSP, formerly the Bulgarian Communist Party), the Union of Democratic Forces (UDF, a coalition formed in 1989 as opposition to the Communist government), and the Movement for Rights and Freedoms (MRF, representing the Turkish minority). The newest major party is the Simeon II National Movement (SNM) founded by former king and prime minister Simeon Saxe-Coburg-Gotha in 2001.

FREE ELECTIONS 45 YEARS LATER

For Bulgarians over the voting age of 18, the 1990 parliamentary elections were a most exciting political experience. Yet the elections were also the cause of profound disappointment. Despite massive public demonstrations of unity by the opposition coalition, the anticommunist votes got dispersed among parties that did not muster the necessary 3 percent of the public vote. The Bulgarian Socialist Party still won the majority of seats in the Grand National Assembly, but Bulgarians did not resign themselves to continued rule by the BSP.

Shortly after the elections students at the University of Sofia went on strike, social behavior without precedent in the history of the nation. The students demanded both an investigation into the fairness of the elections and the resignation of the socialist president, Petar Mladenov, who had called out army tanks in reaction to the widespread demonstrations. The strike spread throughout the country, and before long Mladenov was pressured into resigning. Parliament was in deadlock over the election of a new president since no party could muster the necessary majority.

In the political summer of 1990 a unique movement developed with the aim of forestalling a socialist victory. Led by students and a number of the country's intellectuals, Bulgarians pitched tents in the center of the capital, forming what came to be known as the "City of Truth." Over the next several months the demonstration grew in size and power, numbering at its height 6,000 to 7,000 people.

NATIONAL ELECTIONS

Bulgarian citizens 18 years or older are entitled to vote. Bulgaria's sixth parliamentary election was held on June 25, 2005. The Coalition for Bulgaria, of which BSP is a partner, had a lead with 34.2 percent of votes, but did not have a majority. The ruling party, SNM, was second, with 21.9 percent. Third was MRF, with 13.7 percent.

The presidential elections held on October 26, 2006, saw incumbent president Georgi Purvanov winning another five-year term in office. Parvanov, a former leader of the BSP, became the first Bulgarian president to win reelection since the fall of Communism in 1989. He has enjoyed wide popularity, mainly because of his pro-European views, and formally presided over the country's entrance to the EU in January 2007.

In the 17 years since the collapse of Communism in 1990, Bulgaria has managed to strengthen its democratic governance system with a stable parliament, reliable government structures, an active civil society, and a free media.

ECONOMY

THE COLLAPSE OF THE BERLIN WALL in 1989 ushered in change throughout Eastern Europe. In Bulgaria the socialist economy collapsed and the country was impelled to reform its centralized economy into a free-market economy.

The socialist system had left the country with an unwieldy economic structure and a daunting national debt. It had concentrated too much on heavy industry while lacking energy supplies and natural resources. As a result, and due also to chaotic management, in the early and mid-1990s there was a steep drop in agricultural and industrial productivity. Inflation and unemployment rates skyrocketed.

Above: **The harbor in the Black Sea port of Varna.**

Opposite: **A worker holding a harvest of strawberries at the Pavel Banja cooperative farm in Bulgaria.**

MAJOR REFORMS

The new government embarked on a series of economic reforms in 1991, based on monetary "shock therapy." Inflation was curbed by a drastic increase in all prices and interest rates, and by withdrawing state subsidies from ineffective enterprises. While these measures did eventually succeed in stabilizing the annual inflation rate, they badly sidelined the country's economic development and reduced the living standards of the people.

With international support Bulgaria adopted further reforms in 1997 that included major trade and price liberalization, social sector reforms, establishment of a currency board, and divestiture of state-owned enterprises. This successfully turned around Bulgaria's economy, lowered inflation, and boosted investor confidence. The private sector has also grown rapidly, contributing to 64 percent of the country's gross domestic product (GDP) in 2004.

In 2003 the EU declared Bulgaria a fully functioning market economy. In 2005 Bulgaria's GDP growth rate was 5.5 percent. The government's recent efforts have been focused on reducing taxes, curbing corruption, and increasing foreign investment. Bulgaria's unit of currency is the lev, which has been pegged to the euro since 1999.

INDUSTRY UNDER COMMUNIST RULE

Before World War II industrial enterprises were mostly those of textile production, food processing, and woodworking. There was no heavy industry to speak of, as power sources and technical facilities were rudimentary. After the war, under Soviet influence, the economy was reorganized after the Soviet model and became tied to it.

Bulgaria wanted to catch up with the industrialized nations by setting up heavy industry. It concentrated on heavy machinery production and on chemical and metallurgy plants, even though the country lacked both natural resources and export markets. At the same time, the government curtailed the development of light industries, mainly consumer products, despite the fact that the country had considerable experience and a good international reputation in that area.

The price it had to pay was high. Bulgaria could not afford to keep up with the latest technological developments in heavy industry. Nor could it compete in the international market on price and quality. Its huge plants soon became outdated. To upgrade them, the government had to resort to high-interest loans, which added to the fast-growing national debt.

Mothers of small children turn up in force at an anti-pollution rally in Sofia, protesting against the dangers of high levels of industrial waste.

21ST-CENTURY INDUSTRY

Today, in the 21st century, industry contributes 30.4 percent of the GDP. Since the major economic crisis of 1997, the government has been committed to economic reform and fiscal planning. Bulgaria's industrial sector has grown slowly but steadily in the early 2000s. Low inflation and structural reforms have improved the business environment and attracted direct foreign investment.

The performance of individual industries has been varied. Food and tobacco processing, together with the electronics industry, suffered from the loss of Soviet markets and have not been able to compete in Western Europe. Bulgaria's textiles and clothing exports, on the other hand, have performed well in both domestic and international markets.

Oil refining survived the 1990s because of a strong export market and the takeover of Burgas Refinery by Russian oil giant LUKoil. The chemical

A factory in central Bulgaria. Heavy industry, once promoted and developed to the neglect of light industry, is now virtually immobilized.

industry has also done well but is subject to fluctuating natural gas prices. Mining, however, has declined. Bulgaria is rich in minerals such as copper, gold, iron, lead, and zinc, but many deposits remain unexcavated because of a lack of modern equipment and funding.

The construction industry met with a downturn in the 1990s when industrial and housing projects declined, but made a recovery in the early 2000s. The sector, now dominated by private companies, has resumed the foreign building programs that led to prosperity in the Communist era. Shipbuilding has prospered, too, because of foreign ownership and privatization.

FISHING

Bulgaria's fishing industry remains in transition from a centralized economy to a private sector market economy. Fisheries production comes from two main sources: the Danube River and the Black Sea. In 2000 there was a 45 percent drop in marine catches. Although the fish-farming industry (particularly sturgeon) expanded in the early 2000s, the catch from both sources has decreased sharply in recent years, yielding only a few species of fish for domestic markets in 2004. Bulgaria now imports increasing amounts of fish.

AGRICULTURE

Bulgaria's traditionally strong agricultural sector has been hampered by slow reform of the deposed Communist system. Under Communist rule Bulgaria's agriculture was heavily centralized, integrated with agriculture-

An orchard in southern Bulgaria. Only a small proportion of the country's arable land is being cultivated.

Tobacco leaves hung to dry. Oriental tobacco is a major export.

related industries, and state run. The estates of large landowners were seized and nationalized, and smaller landowners and stockbreeders were forced into agricultural cooperatives.

To resolve the crisis and return the land to its previous owners, the Bulgarian parliament voted in a new Law of the Land in 1992. This law created a free market, with the aim of allowing landowners to buy and sell land and to form associations and corporations. Few Bulgarians, however, have been given back their land and even fewer have found the means to cultivate the land that has been returned.

Bulgaria has fertile soil and a mild climate, but only some 2 percent of its arable land is devoted to permanent field crops such as wheat, corn, and barley. Other crops include sugar beets, sunflowers, tobacco, fruits, and vegetables. Tomatoes, cucumbers, and peppers are the major vegetable exports. Bulgaria is also the world's fourth largest tobacco exporter. Livestock includes cattle, sheep, poultry, pigs, and buffaloes. The main dairy products are yogurt and white cheese.

SERVICES

The services sector is the largest contributor to the GDP at 60.3 percent. In 2005 the labor force was estimated at 3.3 million; some 56.3 percent worked in services, 32.7 percent in industry, and 11 percent in agriculture. Growth has been concentrated in government services, although the quality and kinds of services vary greatly. The Bulgarian banking system was completely reformed in the 1990s and fully privatized in 2003. The tourism industry has also grown rapidly since the early 2000s. In 2004 over 4 million tourists visited Bulgaria, compared with 2.3 million in 2000. Most of the tourism industry had been privatized by 2004.

Yellow trams are a familiar sight on the streets of Sofia.

TRANSPORTATION

Bulgaria has a modern and efficient transportation system. Because international commercial routes cross the Balkan Peninsula, connecting Europe with Asia and Africa, comprehensive rail and road systems have been developed in Bulgaria.

There are also 132 airports with paved runways, as well as maritime transportation along the Danube River and across the Black Sea.

TRAVEL BY TRAIN Most of the country's railroad system was built before World War II. By 2002 the railways totaled 3,967 miles (6,384 km). Sofia is the hub of both domestic and international rail connections. Large cities are connected by express trains. Freight transportation is also big business; in 2001, 83 percent of railroad revenue came from freight charges. Most Bulgarians prefer to travel by train as it is cheap and reliable.

ROADS In Bulgaria, there are 63,392 miles (102,020 km) of roads. Two international highways pass through Bulgaria, and a major highway runs from Sofia to the Black Sea coast. There are plans to upgrade the roads and integrate the system into the European grid. The focus is on improving road connections with Turkey and Greece, and domestic connections linking Sofia, Plovdiv, and Burgas.

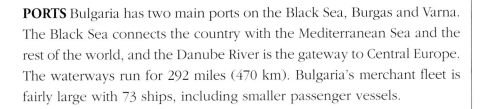

A lone car on one of Bulgaria's better roads.

PORTS Bulgaria has two main ports on the Black Sea, Burgas and Varna. The Black Sea connects the country with the Mediterranean Sea and the rest of the world, and the Danube River is the gateway to Central Europe. The waterways run for 292 miles (470 km). Bulgaria's merchant fleet is fairly large with 73 ships, including smaller passenger vessels.

AIRPORTS AND AIRLINES Bulgaria has three international airports—in Sofia, Varna, and Burgas. Sofia Airport is the oldest and largest, and has the busiest air traffic. The national airline company is Bulgaria Air, which flies to most major European cities.

ENVIRONMENT

WHEN BULGARIA'S HEAVY INDUSTRIES were being vigorously set up in the Communist era, nobody considered the threat they might one day pose to the environment.

The air in Bulgaria's cities was polluted from industrial and vehicular emissions; the rivers were full of raw sewage, heavy metals, and detergents; the forests were scarred by acid rain, which resulted from air pollution; and once-fertile soils had been contaminated with heavy metals from metallurgical plants and other industrial wastes.

The ecological balance was also badly disturbed. Over 40 percent of Bulgaria's population lived in areas with dangerous levels of pollution. The situation used to be grave in Devnya, Plovdiv, Varna, Elisseina, Kurdzhali, and Pirdop, where sulfuric oxide emissions were more than three times the permissible limit. Local residents saw a serious rise in respiratory and other pollution-related diseases, with children being the worst affected.

IN THE NAME OF PROGRESS

Like other Soviet countries, Bulgaria saw unrestrained industrial development as the pathway to national advancement and progress toward the socialist ideal. The extent of damage done to the environment was not addressed until the government of Todor Zhivkov (1962–89) was overthrown in 1989.

The Zhivkov government's commitment to its industrial policy and the lack of funds for protective measures forced it to conceal major environmental hazards. Plants and factories that failed to meet environmental standards paid only token fines, and the government had no real incentive to institute changes.

Opposite: **The picturesque Balkan Mountains National Park is a protected area in the Maliovitsa region of Bulgaria.**

A lack of environmental planning and control under the past Communist rule has taken a toll on Bulgaria's cities.

Although environmental awareness has improved in present-day Bulgaria, the state's lack of administrative strength and fears of unemployment have prevented it from clamping down on many dangerous practices.

GLOOMY SKIES

None of Bulgaria's major cities has escaped intense air pollution, with Sofia being the worst, as ever-increasing numbers of cars contribute to the smog. The problem stems from the combined emissions of industry, transportation, and energy production.

In the mid-1990s, Bulgaria was among the 50 countries with the highest industrial emissions of

A steam train traveling in the outskirts of Sofia.

carbon dioxide. Airborne pollutants, causing defoliation of natural forest cover, have damaged an estimated 25 percent of Bulgaria's forests.

TRANSPORTATION Some 70 to 80 percent of Sofia's air pollution is caused by vehicular emissions. In the 1990s, a rapid increase in motor vehicles using leaded fuel exacerbated the problem. Transportation generated 45 percent of total nitrogen oxide emissions, 39.5 percent of carbon oxide emissions, and 13.4 percent of carbon dioxide emissions.

In the early 2000s, however, Sofia began to phase out the use of leaded fuel following the Environment for Europe (EFE) Conference initiatives. Besides promoting the use of unleaded gasoline throughout the region, the Sofia Initiatives established during the conference also aimed at significantly reducing sulfur and particulate emissions.

ENERGY PRODUCTION A major source of toxic emissions comes from thermoelectric power stations. Low-quality brown lignite coal remains the main resource for energy and heat production in Bulgaria. Because of its high sulfur and ash content, lignite is responsible for 83 percent of the total emissions of sulfuric oxides.

Burning coal for electricity releases sulfur dioxide and nitrogen oxide into the air, causing acid rain. Forests, trees, lakes, animals, and plants all suffer from the effects of acid rain. Acid rain can make trees lose their leaves, damage their bark, and stunt their growth. Fish that live in the lakes and rivers polluted by acid rain are poisoned, and birds can die from eating the toxic fish. Human health may be affected too.

In comparison with European standards, Bulgarian industrial technology is characterized by exceptionally low energy efficiency. To make matters worse, there is a high proportion of the more energy-intensive industries, causing Bulgaria to use many times more energy than average European countries in order to produce every dollar of its GDP.

Factories in Sofia giving off smoke and causing air pollution.

47

INDUSTRY Bulgaria has many chemical, cement, textile, petrochemical, leather, and oil refining industries, as well as metallurgical plants and factories that produce construction materials. Every one of them emits high levels of pollutants.

The unsustainable practices of many such heavy industries have created 14 "hot spots," or high-risk areas affecting local health. These are densely populated towns and villages, where more than one-third of the population resides.

The most heavily polluted hot spot is the region of Maritsa Iztok, where 73 percent of the country's total sulfur oxides, 30 percent of the nitrogen oxides, and 65 percent of the methane are emitted.

STATE OF WASTE

Waste generation is inevitably linked to economic and social development. The increase in production, consumption, and per capita income is connected with an increased demand in natural resources and the generation of more pollutants and waste.

Solid waste concentrations in Bulgaria are traditionally very high, and the proportion of recycled waste is small. The most common method for discarding industrial, household, and agricultural waste is to dump it at unregulated landfills. One of the reasons for this is the lack of modern facilities and technology for the processing and disposal of waste, including hazardous materials.

SOIL CONTAMINATION Severe soil contamination and erosion are the result of poor waste-management practices. Industrial pollutants, especially from metallurgic plants and unregulated mines, are responsible for damage to 115 square miles (298 square km) of land. Toxic waste compounds from copper pyrite and lead-zinc ore processing have also degraded large areas of land. In some areas the soil is so badly damaged that it cannot be used for agriculture.

WATER SUPPLY

Shortages of drinking water are experienced by the residents of several regions of Bulgaria. Water losses in the distribution system (up to 60 percent) and high consumption rates by industry (31 percent), together with normal household use, are the main causes of the lack of drinking water.

The European Environment Agency reports that Sofians each use 118 gallons (447 l) of water per day, compared with only 37 gallons (140 l) used in Brussels. Even though widely known, many water-saving measures are not practiced in Bulgarian households.

Another problem is that natural water resources are unevenly distributed in the territory. There are some areas with low water reserves that are next to areas with relatively abundant supplies. Villages are the worst hit, with 33 percent of villagers having no water supply at all.

Waste management is Sofia's biggest municipal problem. The city's waste is dumped into the nearby open-pit sand mines of Dolny Bogrov, which are now filled with water, causing contaminants to leach into the city's groundwater.

A salt lake in Burgas. Many such lakes and rivers near industrialized cities are polluted.

POLLUTED RIVERS

By the early 1990s, two-thirds of Bulgaria's rivers were already heavily polluted, and the Yantra River was classified as the dirtiest river in Europe. Today, in the 21st century, almost all the major rivers and the Black Sea are fouled by factories that dump detergents, heavy metals, nitrates, oils, and untreated sewage directly into the water. The pollution is so severe that the water from the Danube, Iskur, and Maritsa rivers is not even fit for irrigation.

In 2000 only 25 to 33 percent of industrial wastewater was treated, and the country's municipal wastewater treatment plants served only 36 percent of households and 12 percent of towns. Despite the fact that two of the country's largest industrial cities, Varna and Burgas, are located on the Black Sea coast, wastewater treatment facilities remain inadequate or nonexistent. For many companies it is cheaper to pollute than to invest in treatment technologies.

BULGARIA'S BIODIVERSITY

Bulgaria covers a mere 1 percent of Europe's area, but has greater biodiversity than Germany, Poland, or Great Britain. This is due to its extraordinarily varied climate, and its geological and topographic conditions. Bulgaria's natural environment is home to 383 bird species (77 percent of those found in Europe), 207 Black Sea and freshwater fish species, 94 mammal species, 36 reptile species, 16 amphibian species, 27,000 insects and other invertebrates, 200 types of edible fungi, and 3,500 to 3,750 vascular plant species.

The nation also supports a great number of ecosystems and representative communities that are highly valuable both commercially and ecologically. These include Bulgaria's forests, which cover about 9.6 million acres (3.9 million ha) or one-third of the territory of the country.

The government's National Biodiversity Conservation Plan is aimed at conserving, strengthening, and restoring key ecosystems, biological species and their genetic resources, and, very important, at ensuring the sustainable use of natural resources. Species conservation is regulated by the Hunting Act (2000), the Medicinal Plants Act (2000), the Fisheries and Aquacultures Act (2001), and, above all, the Biodiversity Act (2002).

Endemic, or native, plants account for nearly 5 percent of Bulgaria's entire flora (a high proportion compared with other larger European countries). Moreover, 8.8 percent of noninsect and 4.3 percent of insect species are endemic.

THREATS TO BIODIVERSITY

Bulgaria's unique genetic resources are subject to many assaults, including the illegal felling of forests for timber and the destruction of natural habitats. The loss and degradation of both aquatic and terrestrial habitats is the biggest threat, affecting all kinds of ecosystems, ranging from the alpine forests to the coastal wetlands.

Pollution of Bulgaria's fertile soils, air, and water has intensified in recent decades and is devastating to both biological diversity and human health. Virtually all forms of industrial, agricultural, transportation, and household pollution are present in the Bulgarian landscape and threaten biological diversity in varying degrees.

The overexploitation of many economically valuable species has affected various ecosystems and habitats. This includes the illegal gathering and export of fungi, medicinal plants, reptiles, and amphibians; excessive fishing and trawling along the Black Sea coast and open waters; and poaching and sport hunting of mammals and birds (especially waterfowl and birds of prey).

A view of clear blue lakes in Rila National Park.

PROTECTED AREAS

One of the most important ways of preserving biological diversity is the protection of ecosystems and habitats. Protected areas in Bulgaria cover over 1.2 million acres (485,640 ha) or 4.4 percent of the country, and are regulated by the Protected Areas Act (1998).

These areas include 3 national parks, 10 nature parks, 12 people's parks, 475 natural monuments, 125 protected localities, and 90 reserves (including 17 biosphere reserves). The coastal zone is also protected in 12 areas that encompass some 65 percent of the Black Sea coastline.

Bulgaria's three national parks, Pirin, Rila, and Central Balkan, safeguard mountain ecosystems that contain some of the country's most important watersheds and natural resources. The reserves cover a total area of 199,070 acres (80,564 ha), and support forest ecosystems and habitats of rare species, including 60 percent of Bulgaria's total forested area. Today the United Nations recognizes 86 percent of Bulgaria's protected areas and has listed two—the Srebarna Nature Reserve and Pirin National Park—as UNESCO World Heritage sites.

Other high-priority regions for new protected areas or expansion of existing ones are the Rhodope, Strandja, Western Balkan, and Belasica mountain regions; the entire Black Sea coast; areas surrounding and connecting the existing national parks in the Rila, Pirin, Vitosha, and Stara Planina mountains; and the valleys of the Struma and Danube rivers.

ENDANGERED PLANTS AND ANIMALS

In total, Bulgaria has 473 protected animal species and 389 protected plant species. As a result of pollution and human activity, a number of Bulgarian species have become vulnerable or endangered during the last few decades. They include 31 vascular plant species, seven invertebrates, three fish species, two snakes, three birds, and up to three mammal species.

Some examples of rare mammals found in Bulgaria are the Black Sea morik seal, bottlenose dolphin, brown bear, harbor porpoise, and European marbled polecat. Endangered birds include the Dalmatian pelican, ferruginous duck, pigmy cormorant, and red-breasted goose.

An estimated 210 types of fish can be found in Bulgarian water basins. The sturgeon is protected as an endangered species. During the gestation period, fishing for any type of sturgeon within the Black Sea, Danube River, and internal water basins is prohibited in order to protect their population densities.

BULGARIANS

ETHNIC BULGARIANS MAKE UP 83.9 percent of the population; they are traditionally Eastern Orthodox Christians. Turks are the largest minority, accounting for 9.4 percent. Next come the Roma (Gypsies) at 4.7 percent. The remaining 2 percent are Pomaks (Muslim Bulgarians), Armenians, Russians, Tatars, Greeks, Circassians, Gagauz, and many others.

Bulgaria's multicultural and multiethnic society is very much linked to its historical and cultural roots. The "maternal stock" of today's Bulgarians goes back to the ancient Thracians, Illyrians, Bulgars, and Slavs. The Roman, Byzantine, and Ottoman conquerors of the Bulgarian lands also left their fingerprints on the ethnic and cultural makeup of the nation.

Each ethnic group has its own customs and dialects. Some of these date back more than 15 centuries and originated from the tribes who lived in the Balkans at that time.

Left: **A priest at the Alexander Nevsky Cathedral in Sofia. Most Bulgarians are Eastern Orthodox Christians.**

Opposite: **Smiling Bulgarian girls in traditional costume holding bunches of flowers.**

A Roma (Gypsy) with a performing bear. The Roma are the second largest minority in Bulgaria, but they are among the poorest in the country.

MAKING OF THE BULGARIAN PEOPLE

Thracians were the earliest inhabitants of the Bulgarian lands, living as far back as the second millennium before Christ. Then came the Romans. Both civilizations left their marks on the land and its people. To this day there are Roman roads, baths, and amphitheaters in the country.

The Slavs came to the Balkan Peninsula in the sixth and seventh centuries. They were good farmers and stockbreeders. This large ethnic group gradually assimilated with the Bulgars and the Thracians. The Bulgars, who had arrived in the late seventh century, were nomads from the steppes along the Volga River. Of Turanian origin, they allied themselves with the Slavs against the Byzantine Empire, laying the foundations of the Bulgarian state and nation.

A SEPARATE CULTURE

In the long periods of Byzantine and Ottoman rule, the Bulgarian people effectively resisted attempts at assimilation. They succeeded in preserving their language, culture, belief system, and lifestyle. The Bulgarian culture of today bears some Turkish and Greek traces but has largely kept its distinct character.

Bulgarians have shown themselves to be fairly tolerant in ethnic and religious matters, in spite of their country's being traversed by many tribes and peoples throughout its turbulent history. Minority groups generally live in peace and accept each other's differences. Bulgaria is one of the few countries from the former Eastern Bloc where the collapse of Communism did not trigger ethnic bloodshed.

THE PROVERBIAL BULGARIAN CHARACTER

ALTRUISM: Do a good deed and cast it into the sea.

DETERMINATION: The dogs are barking, but the caravan moves on.

FATALISM: If evil does not come, worse may arrive.

FEMALE: A woman is an iron shirt.

FRIENDS: For a lean year, a relative; for a misfortune, a friend.

INFALLIBILITY: God is not sinless—He created the world.

NECESSITY: When there's no work to be found, join the army.

RESERVE: As with the czar, so with fire—go neither too close nor too far.

RESPONSIBILITY: Where there are many shepherds, many sheep are lost.

SELF-IMPORTANCE: An empty bag weighs more than a full one.

SELF-INTEREST: The dog barks to guard itself—not the village.

WEAKNESS: The Greek will fail because he boasts, the Bulgarian because he is pigheaded.

WORK: Work left for later is finished by the devil.

BULGARIAN TURKS

The Turks are descendants of the Ottomans. They are Sunni Muslim by belief and speak the Turkish language. Most of them live in tight-knit communities in the northeastern and south central parts of the country. The traditional occupation of the Bulgarian Turks is agriculture, especially the cultivation of the well-known Oriental tobacco. The social attitudes and customs of those dwellers in rural areas are highly conventional.

AREA OF TENSION Relations became particularly strained in the 1980s. Bulgarian political commentators went so far as to argue that eventual Turkish separatism would give Turkey an excuse to intervene and turn Bulgaria into another Cyprus. Others pointed to the high birthrates of the Turks, raising the fear that Bulgarians would become a minority in their own country.

The rugged individualism of the Bulgarians is reflected in their sayings and proverbs, refined over the centuries.

During the nationalistic campaign of the Zhivkov government, the Turks were given the difficult alternative either of surrendering their cultural identity or of leaving the land they had inhabited for centuries. But in recent years, both sides have shown a high degree of diplomacy in dealing with these tensions. Today the ethnic Turkish party, the Movement for Rights and Freedoms, is a recognized parliamentary power with a decisive voice in the legislative and political life of the country.

LEFT OUT IN THE COLD

Numbering some 370,900, the Roma, or Gypsies, form the third-largest ethnic group in Bulgaria, yet they have little stake in the nation. They speak their own language, Roma, although it has absorbed many Bulgarian words.

The Roma used to live in caravans (horse-drawn covered carts, or trailers) and roamed the countryside. A small number of them still travel in the old-style caravans, and a few keep performing bears even now, hoping to collect a few coins during their stops in towns. Today most Roma live in slums on the outskirts of the big cities. They are mostly illiterate and have an astronomical unemployment rate of 90 to 95 percent. Their life expectancy is much shorter than the average Bulgarian's.

Bulgaria's governments, similar to most governments with a big Roma population, have all failed to deal with the plight of the Roma, who remain at the very bottom of Bulgarian society. Facing abject poverty, chronic unemployment, oppression, discrimination, and exclusion from mainstream society and its expectations, out of desperation many have adopted a life of crime or emigration.

Bulgarian Muslims chat and socialize in a mosque that was recently restored.

WHY THE POMAKS CHANGED THEIR FAITH

The Pomaks are a small group of Bulgarian-speaking Muslims who live in the Rhodope Mountains. They are descendants of Bulgarians who had changed their faith from Christianity to Islam, either voluntarily or by force, during Ottoman rule. There is a rather unusual reason behind their conversion. The Rhodope Mountains were favorite hunting grounds for the Turkish sultan, and Pomaks were often called upon to serve the royal hunting parties. But Muslim tradition stipulated that only believers in Islam might serve the sultan, so there followed a sustained effort to change the faith of these mountain people to Islam.

In one of its cultural campaigns of the early 1970s, the Communist government forced the Pomaks to change their Turkish-Arabic names to Slavic "equivalents." The term "Pomak" was itself banned. Fortunately, no government decree could abolish the cultural traditions of these hardy people. Most Pomaks today still live in isolated mountain villages and have preserved their folk songs, customs, and their old handicrafts of wool weaving and rug making. (*Pictured here is a Pomak concentrating on his woodwork.*)

OTHER MINORITIES

Apart from the Roma and the Pomaks, two other minority groups stand out. The Armenians came to Bulgaria in the early 20th century, driven from their native land in the Caucasus Mountains after mass slaughters by the Turks. They are city dwellers, speak their own unique language, and adhere to their own Armenian Gregorian Church. Traditionally, the Armenians do exquisite craftwork.

The Bulgarian Greeks live mostly in the cities along the Black Sea coast and in the bigger cities in south Bulgaria. They are descendants of old Greek colonists. Although some still speak Greek within the family, their culture and lifestyle differ very little from the Bulgarians'.

POPULATION TRENDS

Since the beginning of the 20th century, Bulgarians were discouraged from having many children. This was because of the inheritance practice of peasants with small landholdings whereby all offspring were given a share of the farm. This led to small parcels of land and large family squabbles.

As a result, low birthrate was the worrisome trend by the time of World War II. Women having to work outside the home also contributed to this falloff. Even government programs of the 1960s and 1980s, offering family allowances and maternity leave arrangements, failed to raise the birthrate.

A mother and her children in a Roma (Gypsy) slum area in Plovdiv.

HOW THE BULGARIAN JEWS WERE SAVED

Few people are aware that the Bulgarian people saved the lives of 48,000 Jews during World War II. Bulgaria was then an ally of Nazi Germany and received territorial favors at the expense of Romania, Yugoslavia, and Greece, but it did not go along with the Nazi pogrom for Jews.

Under German pressure, the government of the day introduced some halfhearted anti-Semitic measures. The Bulgarian population, however, responded with sympathy and support for the Jews. Once, when the Jews of Sofia were to be expelled to the rural death camps, the citizens of the capital stopped the Nazis by preventing the Jews from reaching the railway station, and the Jews were sent home. Subsequently, many citizens demonstrated in front of the king's palace, protesting the official anti-Semitism.

In 1943 the Nazis finally exacted an agreement from the Bulgarian commissar for Jewish affairs to deport 6,000 "leading Jews" to the Treblinka death camp in Poland. But leading intellectuals raised a huge outcry in the media against the plan. Church officials and ordinary farmers from north Bulgaria threatened to lie down on the railway tracks to stop the deportation trains. None of those Jews ever left the country.

The chief rabbi of Sofia was hidden by Bishop Stephan of Sofia, a senior church official, who declared publicly that "God had determined the Jewish fate, and men had no right to torture Jews, and to persecute them."

Faced with such determined and widespread opposition, the government revoked the order, and Jews already taken into custody were released. The day of March 10, the day the death trains were supposed to roll out, came to be known in Bulgaria as the "miracle of the Jewish people."

The population had also become increasingly urbanized after 1945 because of the Communist government's industrialization program. Today around 70 percent of the population is urban.

In 1991 Bulgaria's population had reached nearly 9 million. In 2006 it was only 7,385,367. The decrease was largely because of intensive emigration after the end of the Communist regime.

The size, age, distribution, and ethnic makeup of Bulgaria's population have all been affected by its migration patterns. During the Balkan wars in the early 20th century, genocide in neighboring Turkey, Greece, and Serbia sent huge waves of refugees into Bulgaria.

Migration went the other way, too. Some Bulgarian Greeks left to settle in Greece between 1924 and 1926. In the 1940s many Bulgarian Jews and Armenians moved to Israel and the Armenian Republic. Over 130,000 Bulgarian Turks migrated to Turkey between 1968 and 1978.

The Armenians do exquisite craftwork. They are by tradition goldsmiths, watchmakers, shoemakers, and today, active in information technologies.

Bulgaria's population figures fell further in the years that followed, the result of two big emigration waves. Among those who departed were 300,000 Bulgarian Turks from 1985 to 1989, the result of an infamous campaign by the Communist government. The Turks were forced to change their names to Slavic ones, prohibited from speaking Turkish in public, and even banned from circumcising their sons, which is a ritual required by Islam. Those who protested were forced to leave the country.

Migration both into and out of Bulgaria in the 21st century continues to rise significantly, and such movements are expected to accelerate as Bulgaria became part of the European Union on January 1, 2007. Many Bulgarians leave because they fear that their living costs will soar as the country strives for a European standard of living.

With the falling birthrate in Bulgaria, there will be a larger proportion of elderly Bulgarians.

Bulgaria has a low birthrate of 9.6 births for every 1,000 of the population, while its death rate is much higher at 14.2 deaths per 1,000 (2006 estimate).

BRAIN DRAIN TO THE WEST

Throughout the 1990s and 2000s there has been a brain drain of the country's skilled and professional people. Bulgaria's transition to a market economy and democracy was accompanied by dramatic changes in social welfare, health care, and the cultural sector.

Frustrated by the deteriorating living standards and the hostile conditions for creative work and research, over 700,000 Bulgarians have moved to countries such as Austria, Canada, France, Germany, and the United States. Most of these hopeful migrants are young and well educated.

SOCIAL INEQUALITY

Presently there are two main classes in Bulgarian society—the wealthy and the impoverished. The country needs an established middle class to secure its economic future and political stability. This balancing class, however, has not yet emerged. None of the governments have succeeded in implementing economic strategies to form a strong middle class.

Class tensions are palpable throughout the country, especially since the gap between the very rich and the very poor is constantly widening. The existing economic model in Bulgaria is not based on consumer consumption, earnings, or welfare but, instead, on the level of poverty or, more accurately, on decreasing consumption of economic goods. Some examples of current social inequality include general social dissatisfaction, very limited consumer spending, a decrease in the quality of the labor force, an increase in income disparity, and a decline of quality education and health care.

A Bulgarian couple out strolling, with the man wearing a rather striking orange suit.

Meticulous attention to one's clothing is a long-standing Bulgarian tradition. According to an old saying, "The greeting will measure how well you are dressed, the farewell will match how clever you have been."

DRESSING UP

Bulgarians dress like most Westerners and care about how they look. They prefer natural fabrics such as cotton, wool, and silk. A night out on the town often becomes an occasion to dress up.

Bulgarian folk costumes are richly ornamented with bright, bold colors. Women's costumes include the *bruchnik* (double apron), the *soukman* (closed tunic), and the *saya* (open tunic). Men's costumes are called the *belodresnik*, which means "white dress," and the *chernodresnik*, literally meaning "black dress," but in practice this is more often brown or blue. Present in everyday life, at village celebrations, festivals, or on special occasions, these costumes vary widely from region to region, and their beloved designs are several centuries old.

LIFESTYLE

THE MANY UPS AND DOWNS in the political life of the nation have taught Bulgarians to cultivate and value a stable life among family and friends. They know that close relatives can always be depended on in moments of crisis, to help nurture the young, or to take care of the old.

In public places Bulgarians do not appear to be very welcoming. But once inside a Bulgarian home, that changes. It would be unheard of for a caller not to be offered a drink or a bite to eat, whether it is a friend who has dropped in casually, the person who delivers the mail, or a stranger.

Bulgarians generally do not like the idea of letting the state take care of their loved ones in times of sickness or crisis. If possible, they prefer not to depend on hospitals, nursing homes, or banks. Bulgarians may never think of sending Christmas or birthday cards, but in hard times they will offer their help even before it is asked for. In turn, they will expect the same from others.

Above: **A favorite activity of older Bulgarians—chatting on a park bench.**

Opposite: **Two women enjoying the sunshine on a bench in Koprivshtitsa. Most elderly rural folks have a leisurely lifestyle.**

FEW MIXED MARRIAGES

Bulgarians tend to be strongly conservative in outlook. They do not approve of those who choose to remain single, and they frown upon couples who live together without getting married. A gay or lesbian partnership is totally incomprehensible to most Bulgarians.

Over 90 percent of the adult population of Bulgaria is married. Mixed marriages of people of different races are virtually unknown in this overwhelmingly white society. Even different ethnic groups, or those with different religious backgrounds, do not intermarry. But friendships among all groups are encouraged or, at least, tolerated.

THE FAMILY

Some Bulgarian homes have three or even four generations living together. Such a family often includes grandparents, aunts, uncles, and cousins, too. This is partly due to the acute shortage of housing in the cities.

Bulgarians, traditionally a nation of small-scale farmers and artisans, do not resent sharing their homes with members of the extended family, though middle-aged or elderly parents are more likely to stay with a married daughter than with a married son.

The different generations living under one roof usually get on well together. When two generations share a home, their roles are clearly defined. The younger people usually earn the living, and the older ones tend the home and help raise the children.

Even when parents live away from their adult children, they often act as foster parents for their grandchildren during the summer months. First cousins, who frequently spend vacations together at their grandparents', may grow as close as brothers and sisters. Children often feel closer to their grandparents than to their parents, who are at work all day long and have the thankless task of being the disciplinarians.

The dream home of every Bulgarian is a multistoried house where parents and their adult children's families can each have its own floor and "will not have to change shoes" to visit each other.

A middle-aged couple tending their yard in the outskirts of Sofia. Their children are most likely working in the city.

GRANDMOTHER'S DAY

January 21 is Grandmother's Day, one of the most touching and heartwarming Bulgarian holidays. It is also the professional holiday of obstetricians and gynecologists. In the past the oldest and most experienced woman in the family would help with the birth of her grandchildren. Women today very rarely give birth at home, because trained medical professionals have displaced grandmothers from their function as midwives. But the grandmother's role in bringing up the young ones is still very much evident and appreciated.

Grandmother's Day is a holiday for women. On this day Bulgarian women visit their grandmothers to ceremonially wash their grandmother's hands and to present them with a fluffy new towel. The same ritual is enacted in the maternity wards of hospitals, where nurses are given a towel as an acknowledgment of the nurses' part in taking care of the mothers and their newborn.

Bulgarians believe in hard work and perseverance, but they also know how to party and enjoy themselves.

A young couple in a public park. Bulgarians tend to marry early.

MARRIAGE AND DIVORCE

Bulgarians tend to marry for love. Often they get married when they are young and before their careers are established, so they have little choice but to live with their parents. The high cost of housing also means they are seldom able to move out of the parental home. Children are usually brought up by the extended family.

Except for the Muslim and Roma minorities, most young couples have no more than two children. Stringent family planning is due both to tradition and to economic hardship. Both partners in marriage often preserve a significant degree of emotional and professional independence.

HERE COMES THE BRIDE Weddings traditionally take place in early spring or the fall. Preparations start months ahead, usually with the betrothal, or engagement. In the city betrothal typically takes place at a private party given by the immediate families of the couple. Presents are given, and the couple exchange rings—wedding bands are usually placed on the left hand until the wedding, when they are shifted to the right hand. In small villages there may be a large feast to which the whole village is invited. The engagement period is the time to settle issues of property and money.

Weddings are sumptuous affairs, starting at dawn and often continuing overnight. During the wedding banquet the mock complaint crops up repeatedly that the wine is bitter, so, of course, the only way to "sweeten" the wine is by a passionate kiss of the newlyweds!

Marriage and divorce

When a marriage fails to work, the partners are free to divorce. The court procedure, however, is long and complicated, giving the partners numerous options to reconsider their decision. Nevertheless, divorce rates are rising, especially in urban communities.

The children of divorced parents normally live with their mother until they come of age, when they can choose which parent they wish to live with. The father is usually given the right to spend weekends plus several weeks during vacations with his children. He is also required to pay some money for their support.

An Orthodox Christian wedding in church, solemnized by a priest.

MEN AND WOMEN

Bulgarian women enjoy considerable freedom. This is the result of centuries of wars that took the men away from their families, leaving the women to act as managers and providers.

Socialism has improved the quality of women's education, with laws enacted for the equality of the sexes. State restrictions over earning potential had one effect beneficial to women—it got them out of the house. Families needed two substantial breadwinners, so women had little choice but to go out and work. Bulgarian women, who make up half the workforce, have excelled in their jobs and have proved to be talented politicians, professors, legislators, and administrators. Since 1989 Bulgaria has had its first women vice president and prime minister.

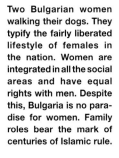

Two Bulgarian women walking their dogs. They typify the fairly liberated lifestyle of females in the nation. Women are integrated in all the social areas and have equal rights with men. Despite this, Bulgaria is no paradise for women. Family roles bear the mark of centuries of Islamic rule.

CHILDREN PLAY THEIR PART

Children are probably the most important members of Bulgarian society. Bulgarian parents will sacrifice anything for the well-being and the future of their children. A child's achievement is a far greater source of family pride than material benefits or professional advancement.

Unless children happen to live with healthy and energetic grandparents, they learn to take care of themselves early. An older child, barely in his or her teens, will often prepare meals and set the table for the younger child and the grandparents. Bulgarian parents expect this and have a low tolerance for waywardness or misbehavior.

Most Bulgarian children remain dependent on their parents right into adulthood. But sooner or later the roles are reversed, and the younger adults start to look after their aging parents. In this way parents and children remain dependent on each other throughout their lives.

Children performing in public to earn a bit of spare cash, for pocket money or for their family.

MARRIED BUT STILL AT HOME It is considered a disgrace if a young adult leaves the parental home before marriage. Unless a promising career is at stake, the parents will be accused of having driven their child away.

Even after marriage, it is common for young couples to live with either set of parents. The young couple might help with utilities and other bills, but most Bulgarians would not dream of asking their children to pay rent. The parents would also contribute toward eventual new homes for their children and help with furnishings and decorations.

A student in class, looking a little apprehensive. Most children learn at least one foreign language at school.

PRIDE IN KNOWLEDGE

Bulgarians believe wholeheartedly in the value of education. The Bulgarian educational system is comprehensive and very stringent, with unique opportunities for study. Competitive examinations regulate access to education. The demand for good education at all levels is so high that even some of the new private schools, where families pay high tuition fees for the students, have introduced such entrance examinations.

Bulgarian education has a long democratic tradition. From the National Revival period of the 19th century onward, Bulgarians have taken pride in supporting their schools. Small mountain villages used to pool together their resources to send their most talented youths to prestigious schools in the cities or even abroad.

School attendance in Bulgaria is compulsory and free. Because of a "tracking" system, the high school dropout levels are very low. The current system of elementary, middle, and high school education, introduced in 1998, has 12 grades in which attendance is compulsory from ages 7 though 16. Students attend elementary school for four years, basic (or middle) school for three years, and high school for three to five years, depending on the course of study. Students who perform well may continue their education at universities after passing the qualifying examinations.

Alternatively, vocational schools offer three years of practical training in a skilled trade. All high schools, except vocational schools, enable students to move on to higher education upon graduation. For adolescents with special talents, a number of high schools provide intensive advanced education in the arts, languages, or mathematics.

About 30 percent of Bulgarian students continue their education past the secondary level. In 2003 the country's literacy rate was 98.6 percent.

ETHNIC SCHOOLS After 1989 secondary schools were created for students with different ethnic identities, thus, for the first time, allowing them to learn two native languages, two cultures, and two religions—Bulgarian and their own native one. Two examples are the Jewish school in Sofia and the Turkish school in the town of Kurdzhali. The idea is based on the understanding that knowledge is the first step toward accepting ethnic differences and "otherness," an agreed-upon official educational policy of the country. These schools embrace a new type of ethos, one that welcomes the mixing of two different cultures.

UNIVERSITIES Colleges and universities train specialists for the professional job market. There are more than 42 institutions of higher learning in Bulgaria, offering degrees at undergraduate and postgraduate levels. They include Sofia University and universities in Burgas, Blagoevgrad, Plovdiv, Ruse, Stara Zagora, Svishtov, Turnovo, and Varna. In 2002 some 215,700 students were enrolled in such institutions nationwide.

College students visit Bachkovo Monastery.

FRIENDS AND STRANGERS

It is hard being a stranger in Bulgarian society. Even in a small village strangers get only a hesitant "hello," and then only after the elderly people, seated on the benches in front of their homes, have looked them up and down. In the cities people ignore each other. Office workers and store clerks appear to wear stone masks.

On the other hand, Bulgarians are kind and generous to anyone who enters their homes. There is a moving Christmas tradition that speaks volumes for Bulgarian hospitality. The woman of the house brings out a Christmas pie stuck with little dogwood twigs that are to tell each family member their luck for the coming year. But before she serves the pie, the hostess sets aside a piece for "Grandpa Vassil"—the stranger who has not managed to make it home through the snow-covered country roads.

Strolling in the afternoon sunshine after a visit to a café or a restaurant is a popular pastime in Bulgaria.

HOUSE AND GARDEN Except for the biggest cities, life in urban and rural areas is fairly similar. There are libraries, youth clubs, entertainment complexes, and attractive restaurants in all the small towns and the villages. Most homes are occupied by one or two families, with front yards planted with flowers and with neat vegetable plots in the back.

Bulgarians are fond of their gardens. Whether they have to travel to the outskirts of the city to tend their plot in a communal garden, or merely step out into their backyard, Bulgarians cultivate their gardens to perfection.

Thriving villages, especially those in the mountains in the south central and southeastern parts of the country, became almost depopulated when people started moving to the cities to work during the industrialization period. The cities, consequently, experienced severe housing shortages. To cope with this, the government started subsidizing housing projects. Today most of the population in the large cities live in these jerry-built and unattractive buildings.

LEAVING FOR THE COUNTRYSIDE Driven by the economic crises of the late 1990s, experienced most acutely in the industrial sector, more and more families began to leave the big cities for a more affordable lifestyle. Life in the countryside is cheaper, less stressful, and healthier, and there are more local possibilities for enterprising individuals. As a result, Bulgarian villages and small towns are once again brimming with life.

Meanwhile, cities and their suburbs are witnessing the rebirth of the one-family home. New Bulgarian houses are solid and beautiful—built to last with deep foundations, brick walls, and red-tiled roofs. When they build a home, most Bulgarians plan it so that a new floor for a future generation can be added on.

A group of lively boys pose in front of a government housing project.

RELIGION

SEVERAL RELIGIONS ARE PRACTICED in Bulgaria, but none very fervently. The 2001 census showed that nearly 82.6 percent of the population is Orthodox Christian. That is, they follow the expression of Christianity prevalent today in Greece, Russia, Romania, Serbia, Macedonia, Syria, Georgia, and in parts of Finland, Poland, the Czech Republic, Slovakia, Hungary, and Croatia.

Another 12.2 percent define themselves as Muslims, 0.6 percent are Roman Catholic, and 0.5 percent are Protestant. There are also a small number of Jews.

These figures represent an overwhelming number of believers, considering that less than a decade ago Bulgarians were described as atheist. But few Bulgarian Orthodox Christians have a clear understanding of the meaning of their faith. Their religion is largely a matter of tradition and is symbolic of their loyalty to the nation.

Above: **A priest conducting a service in the Alexander Nevsky Cathedral in Sofia.**

Opposite: **Church of the Blessed Savior, a small countryside church in Veliko Turnovo.**

FAITH AND POLITICS

During the Communist era the Orthodox Church was pushed to the margins of social life. Religious knowledge was no longer part of the state educational curriculum. The church was banned from its traditional activities, such as running orphanages and hospitals. Religious holidays and the rites of baptism, marriage, and burial were replaced by socialist holidays and rituals.

The constitution of 1971 guaranteed freedom of religious beliefs and rituals, but the state made it very clear to all students and government employees that attending religious services would damage their future and their careers.

Politicians hold a rally, with a strong presence of priests.

ORTHODOX CHRISTIANITY

Religious knowledge had been commonly passed on from one generation to another. But this source was cut off after industrialization in the 1960s and 1970s brought a great many young people from the villages into the cities. The constitution of 1971 also required parents to give their children a "Communist upbringing," and it stipulated that the education of youth "in a Communist spirit is the duty of the entire society."

A RESURGENCE The sustained efforts of the state to inculcate an atheist way of life were by and large successful. The collapse of the Communist regime in 1989, however, led to a revival of Orthodox religious activities. It was no coincidence that the huge rallies of the anticommunist opposition were held in the squares in front of city cathedrals. This choice of venue meant that the democratic movement was once again symbolically connected to the Orthodox Church.

For many centuries the Orthodox Church was virtually unknown in the Western world. Although there have been numerous contacts between the Orthodox, Roman Catholic, and Reformed churches recently, the differences among them are still not clear to many people. In the East and the West alike, Christians believe in the Holy Trinity of the Father, the Son, and the Holy Spirit, and base their dogmas on the Old and New Testaments.

HEART OF THE CONTROVERSY

The churches of the East and the West differ on certain controversial points. These are the very same ones encountered by the church fathers when spreading Christianity in the early centuries of the faith. Eastern theology upholds the absolute equality of the Father, the Son, and the Holy Spirit, and believes that each entity is different in relation to the others. Western theology, on the other hand, emphasizes the unity of God, and that the Holy Spirit proceeds from the Father just as from the Son.

The heart of the controversy between the two churches concerns the administrative hierarchy. The Western side has a monarchical conception of the church, in which the Pope has the authority to rule over the whole of Christendom. The Eastern side, on the other hand, sees Christendom as a community of self-governing churches, without needing to recognize papal supremacy.

Rallies held in front of cathedral squares were meant to relay the message that the church was once again to be part of political life.

A priest feeds the resident lamb of Rila Monastery.

ROLE OF THE CHURCH

The Orthodox Church has played an important role in the building and survival of the Bulgarian nation. The Slavs and the Bulgars who founded the Bulgarian state in A.D. 681 had quite different belief systems, which from the start raised obstacles to their integration. Each of these peoples believed in a pantheon of deities ruled by a mighty god of thunder—called Perun by the Slavic tribes and Tangra by the Bulgars.

Bulgaria was converted to Christianity by Byzantine priests in the ninth century. Ever since, the Bulgarians have insisted on having their own national church, on a par with Constantinople's.

The changes in the practices of the Eastern Church in Bulgaria, brought about by the two theologian brothers Cyril and Methodius, prevented cultural assimilation by the Byzantine Empire. In their everyday teachings, Cyril and Methodius used the common spoken Slavic language as well as their own Slavic translations of the Scriptures, written in the new Cyrillic alphabet.

After the fall of Bulgaria to the Turks, the independent Bulgarian Church came under the authority of the Greek patriarch in Constantinople. The National Revival movement, started within the church, gave the nation back its place in history. This movement gathered pace after the passionate assertion of Bulgarian historical identity by Father Paisiy Hilendarski, a monk from the Chilendar Monastery, in his *Slav-Bulgarian History.*

The first independent Bulgarian schools were opened in the monasteries. In 1870 the Turkish sultan issued a decree granting Bulgarians the right to organize a Bulgarian Orthodox Church. As the first Bulgarian national institution in the Ottoman Empire, the Orthodox Church played an important role in the movement for national liberation.

THE BOGOMIL INFLUENCE ON RELIGION

One of the most popular Christian movements was started in the 10th century by the Bogomils and spread quickly into Asia Minor, Serbia, and Bosnia. The trend gathered momentum and deeply influenced medieval religious groups in Central and Western Europe—the Cathari in Italy, the Albigenses in France, and the Hussites in Bohemia (today's Czech Republic).

Named after its founder, Father Bogomil, the movement was directed against "earthly rulers and injustices," namely the feudal lords, the official church, and the king. It was born out of the despair of the peasantry, because the successors of Czar Simeon had plunged the country into political and social disarray.

The Bogomils believed that the physical world was the creation of the devil. They lived in communes of believers and practiced strict sexual abstinence. They proclaimed direct communion between the believer and God, honoring neither the cross nor the icons, and fiercely attacked the social and political order in medieval Bulgaria. They were persecuted by the state but survived as a movement for several centuries.

REVIVAL OF RELIGIOUS LIFE

The Communist regime is partly to blame for the nation's lack of interest in Christianity, having severely discouraged anyone with a religious vocation, that is, a calling to holy orders. A revival of religious life has been taking place in Bulgaria, however, since the emergence of democracy in 1989. The Bulgarian Orthodox Church now has some 6.5 million members, with 2,600 parishes guided by 1,500 parish priests. It also runs 120 monasteries in Bulgaria with about 200 monks and nuns.

There has been a split between church leaders who came to power in the Communist era and the younger religious leaders of the democratic movement. The newer group wants a change and accuses the older church leaders of corruption and the promotion of Communist interests. But this group is in turn accused of blindly serving today's political powers.

A river baptism in a small town, a testimony to the upsurge of religious feelings in the country.

FOUR MUSLIM GROUPS

After Orthodox Christianity, Islam has the second largest number of followers in Bulgaria, with four Muslim groups—Turks, Pomaks, Gypsies, Tartars, and Muslim. The Turks were consistently thinned out by emigration, resulting in a steep drop in the number of imams—the prayer leaders at the mosques.

With very few exceptions the Bulgarian Muslims are Sunnis. Traditionally living in close communities, they maintain a strong sense of ethnic and religious identity. But few Muslims, whether of Turkish or Bulgarian origin, show a strong attachment to secular Turkey.

A beautiful mosque stands in a busy part of Sofia. Bulgarian Muslims are devout in their faith.

Like the Orthodox Christians, the Muslims in Bulgaria had an impoverished religious life under the Communist regime. It was far more severe for the Muslims, since they were also under intense pressure to renounce their faith and to assimilate.

During the Communist era mosques rapidly disappeared from the Muslim villages, with modern buildings taking their place. Pilgrimages to Mecca, one of the Five Pillars of Islam, became practically impossible. A general ignorance of the tenets of Islam, including the Five Pillars, was the result. The Islamic Institute in Sofia started training religious leaders in 1989 after the collapse of Communism.

A Baptist pastor giving a sermon.

OTHER FAITHS

JEWS The Jews in Bulgaria were a well-organized religious community until World War II. Most of them now are Sephardim (Ladino speaking), who arrived from Spain, but there are also some Ashkenazim (Yiddish speaking), who came from countries north of the Danube. The Jews were governed by a central consistory (like a church council) and a chief rabbi in Sofia. Cities with a large concentration of Jews had, in addition, their own consistory and rabbi.

After the establishment of the state of Israel, a mass exodus in 1948–49 left behind only 3,000 to 6,000 Jews, most of them in Sofia and largely nonbelievers. Today only the synagogues in Sofia, Samokov, and Vidin are functional, and they open only occasionally. There are no rabbis and only one cantor (a synagogue official who sings or chants sacred music and leads prayers) in Sofia.

OTHER CHRISTIANS The 20,000 Bulgarian Armenians are mostly descendants of refugees from the persecution of Armenians in Turkey. They are adherents of the Armenian Gregorian Church. In religious affairs they are headed by a bishop who resides in Bucharest, Romania. The Armenian Church maintains close contacts with the Bulgarian Orthodox Church.

The Bulgarian Catholics have a complex history that dates back to the 13th and 14th centuries when Franciscan missionaries established communities in western Bulgaria.

The Protestant community is the smallest Christian group and the one with the most recent history. The first converts were made in the mid-19th century by American Methodist and Congregationalist missionaries in southern Bulgaria.

Both Catholics and Protestants got harsh treatment during the years of the cold war, allegedly because of their ties with "hostile foreign centers" in the West. Pastors, priests, nuns, and lay believers were charged with spying for the West and with spreading anticommunist propaganda. But there has been a marked revival among these religious groups since the 1970s.

The Alexander Nevsky Cathedral in Sofia, built in neo-Byzantine style, is one of the largest Eastern Orthodox cathedrals in the world.

Улица Гурко
Gurko Street
Gurko-Strasse

Тази живописна улица съхранява атмосферата на възрожденско Търново. Това е най-старата главна улица на града с уникално съчетание на природна даденост и автентична архитектура. Тук на 7 юли 1877 година тържествено е посрещнат генерал Гурко начело на руските войски, освободил и Търново. Днес улицата носи неговото име.

This picturesque street still keeps the Renaissance atmosphere of Tarnovo. This is the oldest high street of the town with a unique combination of landscape and architecture. It was here that on 7 July 1877 the Russian army headed by general Gurko was warmly welcomed by the citizens of the newly-liberated Tarnovo.

Die Gurkostrasse bewahrt die Atmosphäre von Veliko Tarnovo in der Wiedergeburtszeit. Sie ist eine der ältesten Hauptstrassen mit einer natürlichen Landschaft und authentischen Architektur. Am 7 Juli 1877 wurde hier General Gurko festlich empfangen, der die russischen Truppen angeführt hatte, die Tarnovo befreit hatten. Heute trägt die Strasse seinen Namen.

LANGUAGE

TO BULGARIAN POETS, their language is sacred, as it has played an important role in defining and preserving national identity. Bulgarian is a Southern Slavic language, related to Slovenian, Serbian, and Croatian. Fewer than 20 words can be traced back to the tongue of the ancient Bulgars, which is believed to have been of Turanian origin.

The main languages spoken in Bulgaria are Bulgarian, Turkish, Wallachian, Armenian, and Greek.

BULGARIAN has absorbed many Turkish words as well as grammatical features of other non-Slavic Balkan languages. It is the official language, spoken by 84.5 percent of citizens, although their mother tongues may be different, such as Turkish or Armenian.

TURKISH is spoken by many Muslims in the south central and northeastern parts of Bulgaria. It is a Turanian language related to the tongue of the old Bulgars but is very different from modern Bulgarian. The Muslims originated from the same parts of Central Asia that were home to the Turkish conquerors of the Bulgarian kingdom in the 14th century.

WALLACHIAN is a dialect of Romanian and is spoken by a significant segment of the population inhabiting the northwest corner of Bulgaria as well as the narrow strip of about 100 miles (161 km) along the Danube River from the Serbian-Bulgarian border to the Black Sea.

ARMENIAN is an Indo-European language spoken by the descendants of the Armenian Holocaust refugees. In the early 20th century Armenians settled in Bulgaria west of the Black Sea. Over 4 million people in the former Soviet Union, Iraq, Lebanon, Syria, Iran, and Turkey speak this exotic language, which has its own alphabet.

Opposite: **A plaque on Gurko Street written in Bulgarian, English, and German.**

These signs outside a coffeehouse are in Bulgarian, but one of them has included an English word, "kiwi."

GREEK is spoken by Bulgarian Greeks along the Black Sea coast and in the south of the country. It is written in a unique script, the basis for the Cyrillic alphabet used in Bulgaria, Macedonia, and Russia.

THE SLAVIC INHERITANCE

The Bulgarians are justly proud of their language. They were the first among the Slavic peoples to create a rich religious and secular literature. And it was the Slavic holy brothers Cyril and Methodius, and their disciple Saint Clement of Ohrid, whom the whole of medieval Europe had to thank for the Cyrillic alphabet. Their invention of Slavic letters and translation of the scriptures into the spoken Slavic language was an outstanding cultural achievement.

Saints Cyril and Methodius had originally devised the Slav-Bulgarian alphabet for the purpose of establishing a Slavic church in Moravia (present-day Slovakia). The church mission collapsed, and the alphabet system would have disappeared along with it except that some of the disciples of the Slavic apostles had found refuge in Bulgaria.

The educational and creative work of these disciples brought forth a golden age of literature and culture in their new country. In the churches and at court the Bulgarian language replaced Greek. The Cyrillic alphabet, along with Slavic liturgy, literature, and law, spread from Bulgaria to Serbia, Russia, and other lands.

Bulgarian became the international language of Slavic civilization, spreading cultural accomplishments and influences throughout the Balkans and northward to Russia. A number of Slavic peoples still use the Cyrillic script, with some minor variations to accommodate phonetic differences.

Bulgarian has an alphabet of 30 letters, with six vowels, two letters for composite diphthongs, 21 consonants, and one letter to indicate soft consonants. It is a melodious language, not difficult to pronounce, but with an extremely complicated grammar. Although Bulgaria is a small country, there are considerable regional differences among the dialects spoken. These concern mainly the sounds of words, but there are also Bulgarian dialects with subtle variations in word choice and even some grammatical differences.

CYRIL AND METHODIUS: APOSTLES OF THE SLAVS

The Greek brothers Cyril and Methodius were experienced missionaries and brilliant church intellectuals living in the mid-ninth century. The younger brother, Constantine the Philosopher, whose monastic name was Cyril, was educated at the school for the children of the Byzantine imperial family. He had a gift for languages and held prestigious positions as professor of philosophy at the Magnaura Palace School and as librarian of the patriarchal church of Saint Sophia in Constantinople.

In their missionary and translating work, and as inventors of the script that was the precurser of the Cyrillic alphabet, the brothers worked wholeheartedly for the enlightenment of the Slavs. They bravely defended their cause in the home of their adversaries—the Holy City of Rome. But their work among the Slavs of Moravia antagonized the German clergy who regarded Moravia as their missionary field. The two brothers were accused of heresy for not teaching Christianity in one of the three holy languages—Greek, Latin, or Hebrew.

They were summoned by the Pope to account for their actions. On their way to Rome they were drawn into a dispute with Venetian clergymen. It was then that Cyril formulated his defense of the use of the Slavic language in liturgy and learning.

A man checks out a book at a stall in a city square.

BODY LANGUAGE

Bulgarians may appear somewhat reserved, yet they often become very animated during conversations. They use their eyes, eyebrows, and hands to emphasize a point or to express approval or disagreement. When speaking, both men and women tend to make physical contact much more often than people in most Western cultures. They also stand closer together and chat in louder voices.

Perhaps most confusing to outsiders is their habit of shaking the head right to left to express agreement or compliance. It thus appears to onlookers that Bulgarians are always disagreeing with each other. What is more, a Bulgarian gently nods his head up and down to signify "no," though this is more easily understood by an accompanying series of clicking sounds of the tongue. To muddle matters even more, there are Bulgarians who shake and nod their heads in the Western manner. On top of all this the Greek minority shares with Bulgarians the same gestures for "yes" and "no," but the Greek word for "no" means "yes" in Bulgarian. Similarly, a waving finger may not signify a threat, but may merely draw attention to a point of importance. Actual disapproval is easily inferred from a string of loud clicking sounds and from raised eyebrows.

Bulgarians greet each other very warmly. It is common among members of both sexes to extend one or both hands to each other, and to exchange a kiss or three on the cheek—even numbers are considered bad luck.

CONVERSATIONS ON THE TRAIN

Nearly everyone in Bulgaria travels on a train at some time during the year. College students and professors, retirees and professionals, soldiers, the unemployed, commuters, and vacationers all travel by train. As a result, a lively cross section of Bulgarian society can be encountered on a train trip.

A train is hardly out of the station when someone will start to talk—perhaps exclaiming about a newspaper article. Another passenger may take out a homemade pie, and someone else may offer some fresh fruit or a drink.

The train is the place to hear the funniest and the most heartbreaking life stories and to share in the happiness, aspirations, love, or tragedy of total strangers. Bulgarians do not hesitate to ask pointed questions about one's marriage, age, professional status, or salary. Two or more conversations can take place simultaneously in one train compartment. By the end of the journey, strangers who would not have looked at each other on a bus or in a café part as friends.

Two young men in conversation outside a café, and a third giving the photographer the universal peace sign.

Students are polite to teachers, taking care to address them formally even when they have left school or college and become friends with their former instructors.

NAMES AND FORMS OF ADDRESS

Bulgarians have three names—the given name, the father's name, and the family name, which can sometimes be the paternal grandfather's name. It is a common tradition to call children after their grandparents, and so the given name of the firstborn son differs from the family name only in its ending. For example, Georgi Georgiev, meaning Georgi's Georgi.

Variations on the grandparents' names are frequent. These may keep only the root or just a recognizable cluster of sounds—as in the case of Ralitza, named after the girl's grandmother Radka; or as in Miloslav, after grandfather Milko.

The family name is the usual form of address at work, preceded by a polite Mr., Mrs., Miss, Doctor, or Professor. When Bulgarians talk to strangers, they invariably use the polite form of address. The formal "you" is appropriate for addressing business associates, unless there is a close working relationship. This is also the mandatory form of addressing one's teachers and professors, even when students and teachers have become friends in adulthood.

When a Bulgarian woman marries, she can adopt her husband's last name, retain her old family name, or combine the two in hyphenated form. Women who marry young usually opt for the traditional choice of adopting the husband's name. But female college graduates now often prefer to retain their family name after marriage, or at least some form of it.

Names, especially last names, can indicate the person's ethnic origin. Typically, last names have Slavic endings, except for some Jewish and Armenian names. Thus the family name derived from the Greek name Stavros has the masculine form of Stavrev and the feminine form of Stavreva.

No Slavic endings are added to Jewish family names—Grinberg, for example—or to the Armenian Vartanyan.

The informal "you" form of addressing someone is reserved for conversations with close friends, family, and children.

These Bulgarian women are likely to have adopted their husband's last name, unlike young female graduates who are opting increasingly to keep their own family name.

ARTS

THE ARTS IN BULGARIA HAVE A LONG history, dating from ancient times. The Thracians, Romans, ancient Greeks, Bulgars, and medieval Bulgarians have all left traces of their unique artistic lives. Every year archaeologists and historians uncover some artistic monument of Bulgaria's past. Tombs with exquisite frescoes and artifacts have been unearthed, and so have Roman baths with mosaics, amphitheaters, statues, and illuminated manuscripts.

A distinctive feature of Bulgarian arts is its strong democratic tradition. Long centuries of foreign rule prevented the high art forms like painting and classical music from developing, as these were traditionally sponsored by the state.

The political ups and downs of the nation have also shaped its visual arts, theater, and literature. Socialist realism, a form of realistic art that glorified socialist values, was promoted as the most advanced form of artistic expression during Communist rule.

Left: **Frescoes made by artists centuries ago in the Bachkovo Monastery, one of the oldest monasteries in Bulgaria.**

Opposite: **A modern street artist painting a portrait in Sofia.**

FOLK MUSIC AND DANCE

Music has a rich and illustrious history in Bulgaria. Traditional Bulgarian music includes folk songs and choral chants in Old Bulgarian for church services. The main instruments used are the *gaida* (bagpipe) and the *kaval* (wooden flute).

Bulgarian folk music has unusual and complex harmonies, lively rhythms, and an irregular beat. It also varies dramatically from region to region. In the Rhodope Mountains folk songs tend to be slow and sad, accompanied by low-pitched bagpipes. In Sofia the tempo picks up, resulting in wild, fast tunes. In the Pirin Mountains the harmonies often rise to unimaginably high pitches.

Bulgarians love to sing and dance, often to the accompaniment of a bagpipe band.

GIFT OF THE FIRE DANCERS

In the remote villages of the Strandja Mountains, in southeast Bulgaria, visitors can witness an unforgettable dance of very ancient origin. On May 21, the day of Saints Constantine and Helena, the local people light huge bonfires. At sunset, when the fires have turned to red-hot embers, the dancing begins to the beat of drums and the drone of bagpipes.

Barefoot men and women, carrying priceless old icons in their hands, start to circle around the embers, picking up the fast rhythms. Then, raising the religious images high above their heads, they step into the fire. The dance is long and ecstatic. At the end, the dancers shake the ashes and the embers from their feet and step out—unharmed.

These dancers are called the Nestinari. Their gift is handed down from generation to generation, inherited as a family tradition. Even so, not every family member has the gift. Performers believe they are protected by their patrons, Saint Constantine and Saint Helena, who trace a safe path in front of the dancers.

The folk dances of Bulgaria are traced back to the long centuries of Ottoman rule. The best known of these is the *horo* (ho-RO), a lively circular dance where the dancers hold hands and swirl around to the wild rhythm of the music.

Also popular is the *ruchenitza* (rah-che-NI-tza), a competitive dance where the best dancers in the village, men against women, challenge each other's stamina and imagination.

The country has many professional ensembles for folk music and dancing, which take these traditional art forms to world audiences. A number of Bulgarian composers, new and old, have been influenced by Bulgarian folk tunes and have used them in their works. Among the nation's leading 20th-century composers were Petko Stainov and Pancho Vladigerov.

Male dancers like to challenge the women in competitive dancing.

Elaborate paintings cover the walls and domes of the Rila Monastery.

MEDIEVAL CHURCH ART

Throughout the country, elaborately decorated churches and monasteries preserve a wealth of Bulgarian medieval art. One well-known example is the ninth-century ceramic icon of Saint Theodore, which invites comparison with the arts of Egypt and of the Syria-Palestine region.

Bulgarians take great pride in the stunning frescoes adorning the 13th-century Boyana Church, located in the Sofia suburb of Boyana. The Rila Monastery is equally famous for its wall paintings by Zakhari Zograph and other important icons painted between the 14th and 19th centuries. Also on display in Sofia's Alexander Nevsky Memorial Cathedral are over 300 Orthodox iconic paintings, some a thousand years old.

Most Bulgarian icons date from the Ottoman period when Christianity, once the stronghold of state power, became the faith of the oppressed. These small paintings, usually on wooden panels, are often austere and mystical stylizations, rendered in both vibrant and dark colors, often used in daily devotions at home.

The Bulgarian icon became more expressive during the National Revival period. Its distinctive features include an interest in human personality, dramatic detail, and landscape elements.

Icon painters, goldsmiths, wood carvers, and other artisans blended Islamic art with Western European styles and the Balkan art of icon making. They developed their own schools, each with a distinctive style. The Bulgarian religious art of the 18th and 19th centuries expressed a marked confidence in artistry.

LITERATURE

The earliest Bulgarian literature was written in medieval times and can be traced to the ninth century, when Saints Cyril and Methodius created an alphabet for Old Bulgarian, which is the basis of the Old Church Slavonic language. It was a major literary language of Europe, and the Cyrillic alphabet and script were later adopted by Russia and Serbia.

Most of these writings, produced between the ninth and 14th centuries, consisted of historical chronicles and translations of religious works. Some of the most important works were produced during the National Revival period in the 19th century. At that time, Father Paisiy's *Slav-Bulgarian History* became the handbook for the Bulgarian Enlightenment. Among the best-known writers was the poet, novelist, and playwright Ivan Vazov, whose works detailed Bulgarian oppression under Ottoman rule. His writings defined much of the Bulgarian character and influenced many generations of Bulgarian writers.

ZOGRAPH: ICON PAINTER OF VISION

Zakhari Zograph was one of the most talented painters from the Samokov school of iconographers. His secular and realist paintings in the early 19th century were among the most influential works of that time in Bulgaria. Zograph had no formal art education in European schools, but he studied Western engravings and paintings in his father's collection. He came from an artistic family—a brother of his painted the scenes of the Apocalypse in the Rila Monastery.

His frescoes adorn the walls of dozens of Bulgarian churches. He seemed to be spurred on by the image of the wheel of life, which he painted in the monasteries of Preobrazhenie and Troyan. He was consumed by a compulsion to fulfill his creative potential before the wheel lowered him into the open jaws of the monster in his paintings.

The frescoes of Zograph illustrate dramatic biblical scenes, but they also depict the daily lives of ordinary people of the Bulgarian towns and villages. The highest compliment to his talent was an invitation to paint in the cathedral church on holy Mount Athos.

The Ivan Vazov National Theater of Bulgaria, an imposing presence in Sofia, was named after a prominent Bulgarian writer.

ART OF SATIRE

Bulgaria has a strong theatrical tradition, alive to the political pulse of the nation. The first theatrical performances in Bulgaria took place on the stages of the popular library clubs during the middle of the 19th century. They were organized by schoolteachers and educators, and were intended to stir national consciousness and spur on the people to fight for independence and social justice.

The first whiff of the liberating spirit of perestroika—Mikhail Gorbachev's program of liberalization and restructuring of the Soviet system—in Bulgaria came from the theater and the cinema. Playwrights, scriptwriters, and film producers worked out a symbolic language that eluded government censorship. Their works, complete with philosophic and moral parables, allowed them to launch attacks on the regime of the day in the form of bitter political satires. The cinemas and theaters of Bulgaria became the first venues where government propaganda gave way to free thinking.

In modern times the theater continues to be a popular form of entertainment. Modern foreign dramas, as well as both traditional and contemporary Bulgarian plays, including those by Ivan Vazov and poet Peyo Yavorov, take center stage.

IMPOSSIBLE ACTS

Cultural policies under Communist rule enforced an official culture based on Communist ideology. The period between 1977 and 1981 marked the pseudo "golden age" of Bulgarian art, when state support was exceptionally generous but artistic production was tightly controlled, with severe penalties for transgression.

The government suppressed freedom of speech and controlled public art and literature with rigid censorship. Fortunately, intellectual and political dissent never entirely disappeared from artistic life.

In the 1980s cultural funding from the state dwindled until it practically stopped. Suddenly freed from the censorship mechanism but with no financial support, Bulgarian artists started forming small collectives to share production costs. Groups such as the Society for Art in Action and the City Group came into being on the cultural scene.

Artists were willing to experiment and to be politically involved—they worked with unconventional materials, exhibited in unusual places, and integrated exhibition with performance. Totalitarian controls over art finally ended with the fall of Communism in 1989, and artistic expression has since reemerged.

One of the most outstanding 21st-century Bulgarian artists is Christo, a sculptor known worldwide for his technique of wrapping famous buildings and monuments in fabric and plastic and, most recently, "The Gates" in New York City's Central Park.

A movie theater in Plovdiv, showing both Bulgarian and Western films.

101

The Shumen Fortress, over 3,000 years old, included civil and religious buildings within its defensive walls.

ANCIENT DIGS

Bulgaria is a paradise for archaeologists. Because it is the site of several ancient civilizations, excavations are taking place all the time—in the countryside, in Bulgarian cities that rest atop ancient foundations, and even in the coastal waters of the Black Sea.

KAZANLUK TOMB Two thousand years ago the thriving civilization of the Thracians was subdued by Roman legions. The tomb of a Thracian tribal chief, built in the third century B.C., was discovered in 1944 in the city of Kazanluk. The leader was buried along with all the finery and decorated weapons that he might need in the afterlife.

The craftsmanship of the Thracian masters is especially evident in the perfectly preserved frescoes. Human and animal figures, painted in vibrant colors, look as if they are about to step off the wall. The chief and his wife are portrayed as touching each other tenderly.

PLOVDIV AMPHITHEATER People hardly dare dig foundations for new buildings in the center of Plovdiv fearing they might damage valuable ancient artifacts. One such rare find, on the outskirts of the Old Town, is a huge amphitheater built in Roman times. The structure is perfectly preserved—from the stage to the most distant row of seats. Today Bulgarians can enjoy plays in this amphitheater under the summer sky, overlooking the historical hills of ancient Plovdiv.

The Roman amphitheater in Plovdiv, where drama companies still like to stage their plays.

LEISURE

BACK FROM A DAY'S WORK, Bulgarians do not kick off their shoes and relax. Instead they promptly busy themselves with tasks around the house. There is an old Bulgarian saying, "It's fine to work in vain, but not to sit around in vain." Later in the evening they prefer to read books or newspapers rather than to watch television.

In the countryside when Bulgarian women get together, they are likely to bring some work along with them. A leisurely afternoon with friends can involve helping each other with a knitting or embroidery project. Or they may help with the cooking for an upcoming celebration.

The leisure pursuits of men traditionally include making wine and local brandy. Bulgarians are convinced that there is no better wine than their own, produced from home-grown grapes and fruits of their own labor.

Left: **A relaxing hour knitting on the front porch. Bulgarian women are fond of spending their leisure time doing some sort of useful handiwork.**

Opposite: **Bulgarians relaxing on benches and having a leisurely stroll in front of the Ivan Vazov National Theater.**

WEEKEND ACTIVITIES

Making wine is a favorite weekend communal activity in the fall. Friends rally round to help, taste each other's products, tell stories, and sing songs. The men may also indulge in a game of cards or backgammon.

Gardening is another popular weekend pursuit. This is considered a hobby, rather than work. Residents in small towns and villages have little vegetable gardens in their backyards, while those in the cities travel to the outskirts or to summer houses in the countryside to tend their gardens.

Bulgarians are perfectionists when it comes to gardening. Along the Black Sea coast, little family vineyards get just as much loving attention as the largest ones in the land.

Bulgarian men playing a game of backgammon.

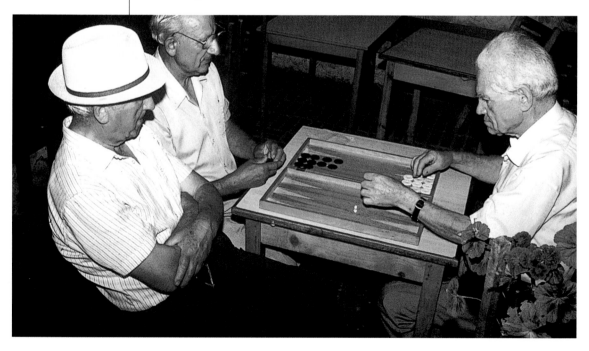

COFFEE, COFFEE EVERYWHERE

Bulgarians drink coffee at all hours of the day and especially in the late afternoon. On weekends city dwellers stroll along streets dotted with small cafés, each with its own distinct atmosphere and faithful clientele.

Some of the cafés are like social clubs, where lawyers, actors, university professors, writers, artists, and people in the film industry each have their chosen corners.

Next to dropping in at a coffeehouse, Bulgarians love to visit friends and relatives. They take flowers and perhaps a bottle of homemade wine for their hosts. These days, however, because of their busy lifestyle, it is usually some special occasion that has them knocking on someone's door.

Apart from public holidays, important festive days are birthdays and name days—the days devoted to patron saints in the Eastern Orthodox Christian calendar. It is a mark of social prestige to be remembered by a lot of people on that day.

Coffeehouses are favorite places for relaxing, exchanging news, and renewing friendships or old contacts. For decades, cafés in Bulgarian cities have been magnets for professionals, students, and retirees.

A typical scene on the beach in summer. Young Bulgarians like to flock to the Black Sea coast whenever they can.

TO THE BEACH AND MOUNTAINS

In July and August most Bulgarians leave their towns for vacations. Theaters and concert halls close for the summer, the cities grow hot and dusty, and school is out. Families with relatives living on farms in the countryside may visit and help with the fieldwork.

The most popular vacationing places remain the mountains and the Black Sea coast. Their numerous resorts offer camping sites, shelters, and chalets for people of all tastes and incomes.

The Black Sea coast, with its warm clear water and sandy beaches, with adjacent forests and river deltas and spectacular vegetation, is by far the best-loved vacation area for most Bulgarians. They go there to relax, camp, swim, fish, and row. But those who live by the sea usually spend their vacations in the mountains—green and cool, with crystal-clear lakes, modern resorts, and well-marked hiking trails.

FAVORITE SPORTS

The Bulgarian mountains are also popular in the winter months. The biggest mountain resorts are in the Rila and Rhodope mountains and at Mount Vitosha. Good snowfalls and snow cover that lasts up to 180 days of the year provide excellent skiing conditions.

Young people of Bulgaria, especially those from Sofia, enjoy skiing. The city is located at the foot of Mount Vitosha, only a half-hour drive from excellent ski and toboggan runs.

Other sports beloved by Bulgarian youth are soccer and basketball. Little boys, whether from a city or a small village, learn to kick a soccer ball almost as soon as they can walk. Soccer games are always well attended, and the country's soccer players are universally popular celebrities.

Men and women doing outdoor aerobics.

When the Bulgarian soccer team defeated the might of Germany in the quarterfinals of the 1994 World Cup, the response back in Bulgaria was tremendous and a spectacular rally was held in Sofia.

Basketball, a recent arrival in the country, is more popular in the cities. Schoolchildren, both girls and boys, play this game.

Other favorites include volleyball, rowing, rhythm gymnastics, track events, wrestling, and weightlifting. Generations of Bulgarian athletes have excelled at these sports in international competitions.

LAUGHING IT OFF

When things get tough for Bulgarians, they respond with an avalanche of jokes, perhaps over a game of cards or a short coffee break. Jokes also liven up family dinners. Bulgarians are especially good at making fun of what scares and upsets them but over which they have no power to change.

NEWSPAPERS AND NOVELS

Bulgarians love to read. The daily newspapers became everybody's favorite reading material for about two years after democratic changes began. At the time, newspapers were so popular that it was very difficult to find a leading newspaper after 8 A.M. This frenzied hunger for real political news, however, has now been satisfied, and although they still read newspapers, Bulgarians have turned back to their usual fare—novels, short fiction, and poetry. Bulgarians have remained faithful to the book. They read everywhere—on the train, on the bus, and at home in the evenings. Public libraries and bookstores are always full of people. When the weather is fine, book vendors are out in the city centers, with small groups of readers sampling their wares.

The most popular jokes ridicule and highlight the shortcomings of Bulgarians' national character or the inadequacies and follies of ruling politicians.

110

GABROVO: HOME OF HUMOR AND SATIRE

There is a city in Bulgaria that has an international reputation for laughing at its own citizens. It is Gabrovo, an important industrial center in the heart of Bulgaria. It boasts the world's first Home of Humor and Satire, opened in 1974, a museum with extensive exhibitions of humorous items.

The world's only Festival of Humor and Satire was started in Gabrovo in 1965 and has been held there every year since. "The world," the people of Gabrovo say, "has survived because it has laughed."

Here are a few typical jokes and anecdotes that poke fun at the slyness and stinginess of Gabrovo's citizens:

A young man told his father he wanted to become a doctor—a heart specialist. "You fool!" cried his father. "Better study dentistry. Man has got one heart, but 32 teeth!"

Two Gabrovo drivers met on a narrow bridge, but neither would back up, in order not to waste fuel. One took out a newspaper and began to read, thinking the other would soon get fed up and back up. But the other driver got out, sat down on the hood of his car and said, "After you've read the paper, can I borrow it?"

When entertaining guests on a name day, Gabrovo citizens put two or three uncracked nuts on top of a heap of nutshells, both for the sake of economy and in order to let people think that many guests have visited the name-day celebrant.

When renting rooms, they always make sure that they get a window near a lamppost, so that they can make use of that light and not have to switch on their own lights at night.

(Pictured on the left, a man from Gabrovo amuses himself and his customers while having a yard sale.)

At the end of the 19th century, journalist and nature-lover Aleko Konstantinov created the character of Bai Ganyu that has brought many smiles to the faces of the normally serious Bulgarians.

FUNNY STORIES

Bulgarians are fond of telling stories. Their favorite characters are sly peasants, not too polished but daring and witty. Two such enduring figures are Sly Peter, who was created 1,300 years ago, and Bai Ganyu, who made his first appearance in 1895.

There is no Bulgarian who has not chuckled over the adventures of these two comic characters. Sly Peter is adept at outwitting everybody, especially his social superiors and, at times, even himself. Bai Ganyu was originally a smart and ruthless peasant.

Keeping pace with the modern world, Bulgarians have wittily transformed Bai Ganyu the peasant into Ganev the aspiring engineer, who shamelessly boasts of Bulgarian achievements in science and technology.

GANEV HUMOR

At an international fair of new technologies, the Russians exhibited a clock with a little bird that came out on the hour crying loudly, "Lenin! Lenin!" But engineer Ganev got the better of the Russians by exhibiting a very similar clock. Only instead of the bird, it was a figure of Lenin who popped out, crying, "Cuckoo! Cuckoo!"

At a conference of new technologies the American representative bragged that cellular phones and pagers had long been outmoded in the United States. Instead, he said, Americans now use a tiny implant in their fingernail to send and receive information.

The Japanese representative claimed that they too had a similar device—but implanted in the tooth. At this point, engineer Ganev burped loudly but was quick to say, "I'm sorry, I just received a fax."

He tends to say the wrong things, yet some of his blunders are telling comments on his international competitors.

TEN PENNIES AND A CHUCKLE

Here is one of the stories in which Sly Peter scores a point over the *chorbadjia*, the richest man in the village.

Sly Peter and the *chorbadjia* were in a public bath. As soon as the *chorbadjia* finished his bath, he wound a sheet around himself and conceitedly asked, "Peter, seeing me as I am, nearly naked, how much do you estimate I'm worth?"

"Hum," Sly Peter thought for a moment. "You're worth ten Turkish pennies."

"You fool!" The *chorbadjia* was angry. "Why, the sheet alone costs ten Turkish pennies!"

"I know," Sly Peter said calmly. "That's why I said ten Turkish pennies."

FESTIVALS

BULGARIAN FESTIVALS ARE VARIED and lively. Some are Christian holidays, some have pagan origins, and others commemorate Bulgarian historical events. They can involve indoor activities, where families and close friends gather together to feast and chat, or they may be celebrated outdoors in city squares and village schoolyards, in vineyards, or at the seaside and riverbanks. Some have fixed dates, others do not, while some go on for longer than a day.

Opposite: **Performers with huge masks and cowbells tied around their waists are a distinctive sight at carnival time.**

WHEN IT IS TIME TO CELEBRATE

National Holidays
March 3   The Liberation of Bulgaria (independence from the Ottoman Empire)
May 1   Labor Day
May 24   Day of Letters (celebrates Bulgarian education and culture, and the Cyrillic alphabet and Bulgarian press)

Winter Holidays
December 25–27   Christmas
January 1   Vassilyovden (Saint Vassil's Day)
January 6   Yordanovden (Epiphany)
January 7   Ivanovden (Saint John the Baptist's Day)
January 18   Atanasovden (Saint Athanasius's Day)

Pre-Spring Holidays
February 14   Trifon Zarezan (Day of the Vineyards)
February   (Sunday) Zagovezni (Shrovetide)
March 1   Baba Marta
March   (Saturday) Todorovden (Saint Todor's Day)

Spring Holidays
March/April (Sunday) Easter
May 6   Gergyovden (Saint George's Day)
May 21   Saints Constantine and Helena's Day

Fall Holidays
October 26   Dimitrovden (Saint Dimitri's Day)
November   Day of the Souls

THE WANDERING NATIONAL HOLIDAY

Until the "gentle revolution" of 1989, the Bulgarian national independence holiday was celebrated on September 9. On this day in 1944, eight months before the end of World War II in Europe, the Soviet army reached the capital, Sofia, in its advance toward Berlin. An antifascist alliance of political forces, called the Fatherland Front, rose to power, but it was in turn completely taken over by the Communist Party less than three years later.

September 9, 1944, thus effectively became the first day of Bulgaria's socialist era. That day used to be celebrated in the grandiose style of Communist governments—with students and employees parading en masse in front of red-draped platforms, and with Communist Party dignitaries basking in the cheers of the people.

A military parade marching past a government building in Sofia.

After the collapse of Communism, Bulgarians recognized the need for a national holiday that would celebrate much more than a triumph of some political power. The new date picked was March 3, the day of the signing of the San Stefano peace treaty after the Russian-Turkish Liberation War of 1877–78. This treaty reestablished the Bulgarian state after five centuries of Ottoman rule. March 3 symbolized the day when Bulgaria's dreams of national liberty and unity came true, if only briefly.

UNTIL THE STORK COMES

One of the most cheerful Bulgarian holidays is the day of Baba Marta, March 1. The name Marta means the month of March. According to Bulgarians, March is a "female month," since its weather changes as fast as the mood of "old Grandma Marta."

Early on the morning of Baba Marta day, Bulgarians tie little red and white tassels on each other or pin them on their coats with a wish for health, vigor, and happiness. These red and white decorations are called *martenitzi* (mahr-tay-NI-tzi). In the countryside people tie these tassels on domestic animals and fruit trees. The red and the white colors symbolize the blood of the new life that is awakening in the snow-covered country.

Children and adults wear the *martenitzi* in anticipation of spring, said to arrive with the storks from the south. When the first stork is sighted, Bulgarians take off their tassels and tie them onto a blossoming tree.

Red and white *martenitzi* tassels on a tree outside the Clisura Monastery.

LOVE OF LEARNING

In an old tradition Bulgarians celebrate May 24 as the Day of Letters. This holiday was created back in the days of Ottoman rule in the 1800s by the initiative of an ordinary teacher and was embraced with joy and pride by schoolchildren and their parents. Many of the parents—seafarers, artisans, or peasants—were illiterate but harbored dreams of seeing their children educated and making a better living for themselves.

The Day of Letters is an exciting holiday for all, particularly for children who have just learned to read and write. On this day the entire Bulgarian nation pays homage and expresses love and gratitude to the apostles of the Slavs, brothers Cyril and Methodius; to their disciples who founded the first schools in Bulgaria; and to the teachers, educators, writers, journalists, actors, musicians, and artists of modern Bulgaria. Schoolchildren take flowers to their teachers and weave wreaths of ivy and flowers for placement around portraits of Cyril and Methodius.

CHRISTIAN AND PAGAN RITES

Other festivals observed during the year include Christmas, the January winter festivals, spring festivals, Easter, harvest holidays, and the Day of the Souls. Christian meaning is often interwoven with ancient pagan rites.

The Christmas holidays go on for 12 days. They begin with Ignazhden (ig-NAHZH-dayn) on December 20 when, according to Bulgarian folklore, Mary felt her first birth pangs. On Christmas Eve, the last day of the Orthodox fast (November 15 to December 24), Bulgarian families gather around the table for the last vegetarian and nondairy meal of the season. The Orthodox Christmas lasts three days, from December 24 to 26, and religious rituals are supplemented by carnival-like folk festivities. In the evenings groups of young men go from house to house, singing Christmas songs and blessing the hosts.

A similar tradition, called *survakane* (or *survaki*), is observed on the morning of New Year's Day when children visit their extended family and close friends and neighbors to wish them health and prosperity. They playfully "beat" the elders on the back with a dogwood branch that has been tied with a handkerchief and decorations such as dried plums and popcorn. In return the youngsters receive fruit, candy, and money. The dogwood, *survachka* (soor-VAHCH-kah), is chosen both for its sturdiness and because it is the first tree to blossom in the spring.

Buying flowers is a favorite gesture on a festive day such as the Day of Letters.

A performer with his mask off. Festive gear is eye-catching but can be heavy and hot to wear.

FESTIVAL OF THE VINEYARDS

Holidays in February and March anticipate the regeneration of new life in the spring. Although most of them conform to the Christian Orthodox calendar, they have the distinct flavor of pagan times. On Trifon Zarezan, the Festival of the Vineyards, the vines are trimmed in a mood of cheerful celebration and wine drinking. Cleansing rituals that are supposed to banish evil powers mark Zagovezni.

This is carnival time in some parts of the country. On one day, men put on festive clothes, huge elaborate masks, and cowbells, then dance their way through village streets and chase away evil spirits.

The Easter holidays, preceded by Lent and a three-day strict fast for the most devout Orthodox Christians, culminate in church services and rituals that mark the week of Christ's Passion on the cross and his resurrection. For centuries Easter has been the most important holiday for the Eastern Orthodox Christians.

One of the most beloved activities of Easter is the dyeing of hard-cooked eggs on the eve of Good Friday. The first egg is always dyed red and is then put under the family icon, where it remains until Easter Sunday. The next egg is dyed green, the color associated with spring and Saint George, whose day falls shortly after Easter, on May 6. Other colors are also used, and some eggs may be elaborately painted with designs. The eggs are kept until Easter morning, when people rap their own egg against someone else's. The last person to have an unbroken egg is said to have a good year. The whole family gathers around the table for a traditional breakfast of eggs and braided Easter breads, richly decorated with almonds and raisins.

DAY OF THE SHEPHERD AND OTHERS

The springtime holidays, associated with the names of various saints, have a strong undercurrent of ancient pagan rites. The celebrations are wild and boisterous, and entire villages go out into the fields or the village square to dance. A number of rituals are dedicated to young people and to nature. One of the biggest May holidays is Saint George's Day, the Day of the Shepherd. It is a true regional festival in the stockbreeding parts of the country, where people go to the mountains for games and to dance and to feast on whole roasted lambs, pagan rites reaching far back into the peoples' past.

For sheep breeders or shepherds, Saint George's Day is a special occasion.

In the fall there are harvest festivals and rituals commemorating the dead. The day of Saint Dimitar deserves special mention, as it marks the end of the agricultural cycle that began on Saint George's Day. Bulgarians observe the Day of the Souls, or Zadushnitza, by making a traditional dish of puffed wheat and some of the favorite cakes and candies of their deceased relatives. Whole families visit the cemeteries, where they place flowers on the graves of their loved ones and distribute the prepared food.

FOOD

THE LOVE OF GOOD FOOD brings people together in this largely introverted culture. Families make sure they have at least one daily meal together. They would rather have dinner late than to exclude a family member who has been stuck in traffic or is late returning from work or school.

Sunday lunches are usually small family feasts, complete with wine and elaborate desserts. Bulgarians, both men and women, love to cook, eat, and talk about food. There is food at any important occasion, whether it is a party, a celebration, or a commemoration of the dead. Even casual visitors to a Bulgarian home will be given something to eat; if they are houseguests, they will get three excellent meals a day.

Opposite: **A vendor selling his ripe farm-produced pumpkins in Sozopol.**

Below: **A honey stall in a market in Sofia. Bulgarians love desserts made with honey.**

EATING AND DRINKING MANNERS

Lunch is traditionally the biggest meal of the day. It includes some kind of vegetable or meat soup, the main course of a pork, veal, or chicken dish with vegetables (often with a small salad on the side), and dessert. It is usually washed down with a glass of wine, which may be diluted with club soda. Teenage children are allowed to have a glass of light wine with their meals. Bulgarians, who are not heavy drinkers, do not see any harm in this. They believe that if their children are taught to drink in moderation during a good meal, they are unlikely to become alcohol abusers.

Favorite nonalcoholic drinks include various fruit nectars and juices and diluted yogurt. Desserts may be sweet pastries made with sugar syrup or honey, compotes of dried or preserved fruit cooked in syrup, or puddings.

BREAKFAST AND SUPPER On weekdays breakfast is usually a hurried affair. Everyone in the house will simply grab a cup of tea or coffee and a piece of toast, and dash out of the house. Leisurely breakfasts are reserved for the weekend, when pancakes may be on the table or a warm cheese-and-egg pastry or French toast with honey.

Bulgarian suppers are true rituals in relaxation. Lighter than lunch, they start with a fresh salad or an appetizer of pickled vegetables and an aperitif. The most popular aperitifs include *rakia* (rah-KI-yah), the local grape or plum brandy, and *mastika* (mahs-TI-kah), an aniseed-based brandy that tastes like licorice. They are sipped slowly, slightly chilled. The main course tends to be a meat dish, followed by a light dessert, usually fresh fruit or a compote.

A man buys a sandwich at a city cafeteria. As a rule, Bulgarians try to make their lunch more of an occasion than this.

COMPLIMENTS TO THE CHEF

Bulgarians make sure to place all cutlery, condiments, and food, except dessert, on the table at the beginning of the meal. Once everyone is seated, nobody wants to get up again; in fact, it is considered impolite to interrupt the meal to ask for something not already there.

Wolfing down one's food without commenting on its taste is also considered rude. People are expected to keep up an easy conversation at mealtimes and to leave nothing uneaten on their plates. Asking for an extra serving is much appreciated and regarded as a compliment to the cook. A good lunch is often followed by a nap in the afternoon.

Bulgarians are meticulous about the use of a knife and fork. But they sometimes eat fish or chicken with their fingers. Except when eating pasta, they rarely spread a napkin across their laps. Children do that, but adults are expected to eat tidily. Napkins are used to wipe one's mouth at the end of each course or before taking a drink.

INFLUENCES AND VARIATIONS

Bulgarian cuisine reflects many different influences. It may include meats or be vegetarian or based on dairy products. Regional cuisines may recall Russian or central Asian influences, or the cooking of neighboring Yugoslavia and Romania. In fact, as far as cooking goes, there are likely to be more pronounced differences within the regions of Bulgaria than when crossing national borders in the Balkans.

Traditional cooking in the Rhodope Mountains is probably the healthiest regional cooking in the country. It rarely involves frying and uses very little oil, which is usually added to the food only when it has been cooked

FOR THE LOVE OF WINE

Vine growing and wine production have a very long history in Bulgaria, starting in Thracian times. Together with beer and the local brandy, *rakia*, wine is one of the most popular alcoholic beverages in the country. Bulgaria has five distinct viticultural regions: the Danubian plain (north Bulgarian), Black Sea (east Bulgarian), Rose Valley (sub-Balkan), Thracian lowlands (south Bulgarian), and the Struma River valley (southwest Bulgarian).

The quality of Bulgarian wine speaks for itself. Local wines such as Gumza, Dimiat, Pamid, Muscat, Misket, Mavrud, and Melnik are well-known to connoisseurs all over the world. South Bulgaria is noted for its red wines, while North Bulgaria is recognized for its fine white ones. The Black Sea region, with Burgas, Pomorie, and Varna as its three main centers, is where 30 percent of all vines are cultivated. Melnik, in southwest Bulgaria, is a region famed for its full-bodied red wine.

Bulgarians love their wine so much that they celebrate Trifon Zarezan, or Saint Trifon's Day, on February 14, a holiday dedicated to the drink. This tradition dates back to the ancient Thracians and is celebrated nowhere else in the world. Saint Trifon is honored as a patron of the vineyards and is a symbol of fertility in Bulgarian folkloric culture. Vine growers hold vine-trimming ceremonies and perform rituals, celebratory songs, and dances as part of the festivities.

for some time. Rhodope meals, using lots of garlic, nuts, and dairy products, are examples of simple and natural cooking at its best. Marinating, grinding, or blanching the cooking ingredients are not typical practices of this region. The best-known specialty from the Rhodope is *cheverme* (chay-vayr-MAY), a meal cooked outdoors for big family holidays or for town or village festivals. A whole lamb is roasted on a spit, then served with honey and a seasonal salad.

In the Thracian plain bordering on the Rhodope area, cooking methods closely resemble those in Greece. Vegetables, olive oil, and spices are favorite ingredients. Meals are often cooked in several stages. Meats and vegetables are first lightly sautéed, then stewed or baked, and finally topped off with a sauce. The dish of rolled-up grape leaves stuffed with meat and rice known as *lozovi sarmi* (LO-zo-vi sahr-MI) (or dolmas in Greece) is served with a yogurt sauce.

MARINADES AND SEAFOOD

In the plains north of the Balkan range, marinating food is a popular technique. Northern Bulgarian cuisine often uses finely ground meats. Popular dishes include a layered pastry with rice and meat filling, and baked sweet red peppers stuffed with beans.

Residents of the Black Sea coast and those living along the Danube are spoiled for choice when it comes to fresh fish. Bulgarians like their seafood simple—grilled or deep-fried with a touch of lemon. But some holiday recipes call for baked fish stuffed with finely chopped tomatoes, onions, chili peppers, and nuts.

All sorts of fresh fish are plentiful along the Black Sea coast. Fish roe paste is a popular appetizer.

KARVARMA

$1\frac{1}{2}$ pounds (680 g) boneless pork or beef, sliced or cubed
Salt and black pepper to taste
3 tablespoons olive oil or salad oil
1 medium onion, finely chopped
4 leeks, thinly sliced
1 tablespoon tomato paste
1 teaspoon paprika
$\frac{1}{2}$ cup (120 ml) water or $\frac{1}{2}$ cup beef stock
$\frac{1}{2}$ cup (120 ml) dry red wine
Fresh parsley, chopped

Season the meat with salt and pepper and set aside for 20 minutes. Heat the oil in a large frying pan; add the meat and sauté until brown on all sides and well done. Remove the meat and set aside. In the same oil, add the onions and leeks and sauté for five minutes. Add tomato paste, paprika, water or stock, wine, and the cooked meat; mix well and bring to the boil. Reduce the heat and simmer for a few minutes to reduce the sauce. Garnish with chopped parsley and serve with roasted potatoes or salad. This recipe serves four people.

FRIED SWEET CHEESE BALLS WITH SYRUP

For the cheese balls
5 ounces (145 g) cottage cheese
3 eggs
$\frac{1}{2}$ cup (115 g) self-rising flour
1 cup vegetable oil for shallow frying

For the syrup
1 cup (225 g) granulated sugar
1 cup (240 ml) water
1 teaspoon vanilla extract

Place the cottage cheese and eggs in a mixing bowl and mix well. Gradually add the flour while continuing to beat until the mixture is well mixed. Shape the dough mixture into balls with a spoon. Heat the oil in a medium-sized pan and fry the balls until golden brown and crisp. Remove them from the pan, drain on paper towels, and allow the cheese balls to cool. The balls may be cooked in batches.

    Meanwhile, place all the ingredients for the syrup in a medium-sized saucepan, bring to the boil and stir well. Lower heat and simmer for about 10 minutes or until mixture is thick and syrupy. To serve, transfer the cheese balls to a serving dish and drizzle the syrup over the top. This recipe serves four to six people.

A   B   C

ROMANIA

N

1

Vidin

Ruse

**SERBIA AND
MONTENEGRO**

Mikhaylovgrad

Pleven

Danube River

Yantra River

Shumen

Preslav

Vratsa

2

B a l k a n

Veliko Turnovo

M o u n t a i n s

SOFIA

Sliven

Burgas

Tundzha River

*Mt. Musala
(9,596 ft / 2,924 m)*

Stara Zagora

Rila Pl.

Pazardzhik

Plovdiv

T h r a c i a n   P l a i n

Blagoevgrad

Maritsa River

3

Khaskovo

**F.Y.R.
MACEDONIA**

Struma River

Pirin Pl.

Mesta River

Rhodope Mts.

Kurdzhali

TURKEY

GREECE

4

A E G E A N   S E A

D

MAP OF BULGARIA

Aegean Sea, B4	Pazardzhik, B3	Sliven, C2
	Pirin Plateau, A3	Sofia, A2
Balkan Mountains, B2	Pleven, B2	Stara Zagora, C3
	Plovdiv, B3	Struma River, A3
Black Sea, D2	Preslav, C2	
Blagoevgrad, A3		Thracian Plain, C3
Burgas, D3	Rhodope Mountains, B3	Tundzha River, C3
		Turkey, C4
Danube River, B2	Rila Plateau, A3	
	Romania, B1	Varna, D2
Greece, A4	Ruse, C1	Veliko Turnovo, C2
		Vidin, A1
Khaskovo, C3	Serbia and Montenegro, A2	Vratsa, A2
Kurdzhali, B3		
	Shumen, C2	Yantra River, C2
Macedonia, A3		
Maritsa River, B3		
Marmara Sea, D4		
Mesta River, B3		
Mikhaylovgrad, A2		
Musala Mountain, A3		
Nessebar, D2		

Varna

Nessebar

BLACK

SEA

● Capital city
● Major town
▲ Mountain peak

Feet		Meters
16,500		5,000
9,900		3,000
6,600		2,000
3,300		1,000
1,650		500
660		200
0		0

SEA OF MARMARA

ECONOMIC BULGARIA

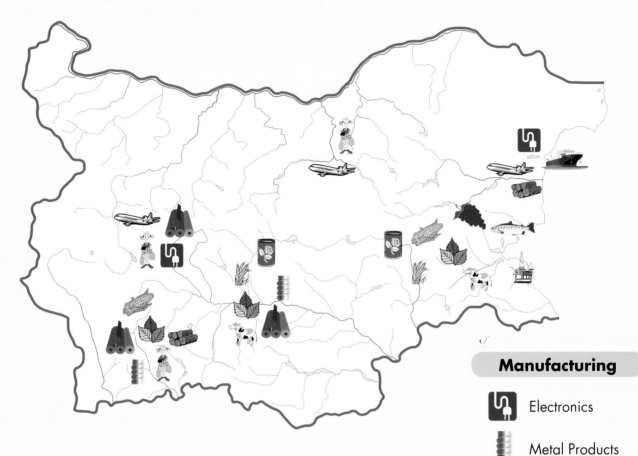

Manufacturing

 Electronics

Metal Products

Textiles

Natural Resources

Fish

 Oil Processing

 Rose Oil

 Timber

Agriculture

 Cattle

 Corn

 Grapes

 Tobacco

 Wheat

Services

 Airport

Port

 Tourism

ABOUT THE ECONOMY

OVERVIEW

Bulgaria, a former Communist country, entered the European Union on January 1, 2007. It has experienced economic stability and strong growth since 1996 when a major economic downturn led to the collapse of the socialist government. As a result, the government implemented economic reforms and responsible fiscal planning. An important industry is the mining of minerals such as coal, copper, and zinc. In 1997, macroeconomic stability was reinforced by fixing the exchange rate of the lev against the German mark—the currency is now fixed against the euro. Low inflation and steady progress on structural reforms improved the business environment. Bulgaria has averaged 5.1 percent growth since 2000 and has begun to attract significant amounts of direct foreign investment.

GROSS DOMESTIC PRODUCT GROWTH RATE

5.5 percent (2006 estimate)

GDP BY SECTOR

Services 60.3 percent; industry 30.4 percent; agriculture 9.3 percent (2006 estimates)

CURRENCY

1 lev (BGL) = 100 stotinki
Notes: 2, 5, 10, 20, 50, 100 leva
Coins: 1, 2, 5, 10, 20, 50 stotinki, 1 lev
1 USD = 1.53 BGL (November 2006)

NATURAL RESOURCES

Bauxite, copper, lead, zinc, coal, timber.

AGRICULTURAL PRODUCTS

Vegetables, fruits, tobacco, wine, wheat, barley, sunflowers, suger beets, livestock, dairy products.

MAJOR EXPORTS

Clothing and footwear; iron and steel; machinery and equipment; fuels.

MAJOR IMPORTS

Machinery and equipment; metals and ores; chemicals and plastics; fuels and raw materials.

MAJOR TRADING PARTNERS

Italy, Russia, Turkey, Germany, Greece, Belgium, France.

WORKFORCE

3.45 million (2006 estimate)

WORKFORCE BY SECTOR

Services 56.3 percent; industry 32.7 percent; agriculture 11 percent (2006 estimates)

UNEMPLOYMENT RATE

9.6 percent (2006 estimate)

INFLATION RATE

7.2 percent (2006 estimate)

CULTURAL BULGARIA

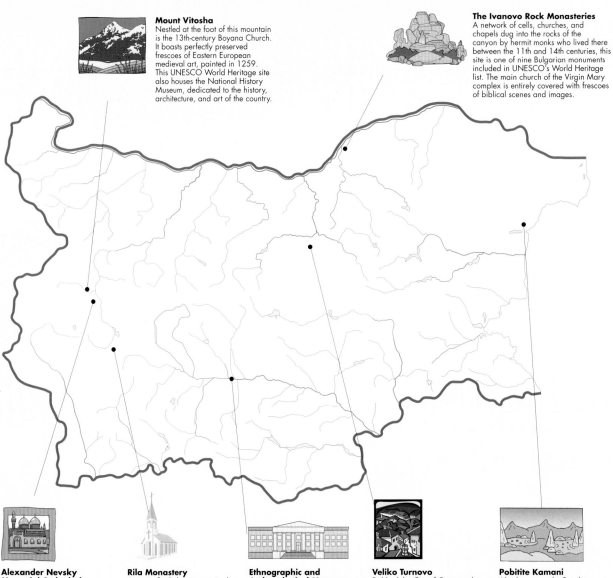

Mount Vitosha
Nestled at the foot of this mountain is the 13th-century Boyana Church. It boasts perfectly preserved frescoes of Eastern European medieval art, painted in 1259. This UNESCO World Heritage site also houses the National History Museum, dedicated to the history, architecture, and art of the country.

The Ivanovo Rock Monasteries
A network of cells, churches, and chapels dug into the rocks of the canyon by hermit monks who lived there between the 11th and 14th centuries, this site is one of nine Bulgarian monuments included in UNESCO's World Heritage list. The main church of the Virgin Mary complex is entirely covered with frescoes of biblical scenes and images.

Alexander Nevsky Memorial Cathedral
Built in 1912 to honor the 200,000 Russians who died in the Russian-Turkish Liberation War, which brought independence to Bulgaria, this is a lavish example of neo-Byzantine architecture. Its museum houses over 300 icon paintings and murals, some a thousand years old.

Rila Monastery
A center for Bulgarian spiritual and cultural life during the 500-year Turkish occupation, this 10th-century monastery is a UNESCO-listed World Heritage site since 1983. It is famous for its wall paintings by Zakhari Zograph, intricate carvings such as the Raphael's Cross, and valuable icons painted between the 14th and 19th centuries.

Ethnographic and Archaeological Museum
Founded in 432 B.C., Plovdiv has many archaeological treasures, including a Roman amphitheater and stadium, ancient fortifications, and Nebet Tepe, a prehistoric settlement. The Ethnographic Museum has lavish displays of locally produced textiles, pottery, and other crafts, while the Archaeological Museum is devoted to Thracian culture and artifacts from as far back as 4000 B.C.

Veliko Turnovo
Dubbed the City of Czars and the "second Constantinople," this was Bulgaria's capital from the 12th to 14th centuries. Situated high above winding river gorges, the town's historic attractions include the Tsarevets Fortress, the 16th-century Church of the Nativity, and the ruins of the Samovodska Charshia complex. In summer the town lights up with a spectacular sound-and-light show.

Pobitite Kamani
Also known as the Fossil Forest, this unique geological site was formed over a period of 51 to 53 million years ago, and was home to the Mesolithic Middle Stone Age tribes. There, hundreds of stone pillars rise from the earth, some up to 32 feet (10 m) high, spanning an area of 27 square miles (70 square km).

ABOUT
THE CULTURE

OFFICIAL NAME
Republic of Bulgaria

FLAG DESCRIPTION
Three equal horizontal bands of white (top), green (middle), and red (bottom)

CAPITAL
Sofia

OTHER MAJOR CITIES
Plovdiv, Varna, Burgas, Ruse, Stara Zagora, Pleven, and Sliven (in order of population)

INDEPENDENCE DAY
March 03, 1878 (autonomous within Ottoman Empire)
September 22, 1908 (from the Ottoman Empire)

ETHNIC GROUPS
Bulgarians 83.9 percent, Turks 9.4 percent, Roma 4.7 percent, others 2 percent

RELIGIOUS GROUPS
Bulgarian Orthodox 82.6 percent, Muslim 12.2 percent, Roman Catholic 0.6 percent, Protestant 0.5 percent, others 4.1 percent

BIRTHRATE
9.65 births per 1,000 Bulgarians (2006 estimate)

DEATH RATE
14.27 deaths per 1,000 Bulgarians (2006 estimate)

MAIN LANGUAGES
Bulgarian (84.5 percent) is the official language and the Cyrillic alphabet is used. Minority languages include Turkish (9.6 percent), Roma (4.1 percent), and others (1.8 percent).

LITERACY RATE
People ages 15 and above who can read and write: 98.6 percent (2006 estimate)

LEADERS IN POLITICS
Todor Zhivkov (1911–98), Bulgaria's Communist dictator from 1954 to 1989.
Petar Mladenov, first president of the Republic of Bulgaria in 1990.
Zhelyu Zhelev, president from 1990 to 1997.
Petar Stoyanov, president from 1997 to 2002.
Georgi Parvanov, current president since 2002.
Angel Marin, current vice-president since 2002.
Sergei Stanishev, current prime minister since 2005.

TIME LINE

IN BULGARIA	IN THE WORLD
A.D. 500–600 Slavs migrate to Balkan Peninsula.	**A.D. 600** Height of Mayan civilization
681 First Bulgarian Kingdom.	
1000–1100 Byzantine rule.	
1352 Beginning of rule by Ottoman Empire.	
1876 National Revival Movement strives toward independence.	**1789–99** The French Revolution
March 03, 1878 Liberation from the Ottoman rule.	
1919 Bulgarian Communist Party (BCP) founded.	**1914** World War I begins.
1943 Bulgaria's King Boris returns from a meeting with Hitler and dies mysteriously.	**1939** World War II begins.
1944 Soviet army invades German-occupied Bulgaria. Soviet-backed Fatherland Front assumes power.	
1946 Bulgaria's monarchy abolished. Communist Party wins election. Georgi Dimitrov elected prime minister.	
1947 A new constitution along Soviet lines establishes one-party state. The economy and industrial sectors nationalized.	**1949** The North Atlantic Treaty Organization (NATO) is formed.
1954 Todor Zhivkov becomes Communist Party general secretary. Bulgaria becomes staunch USSR ally.	**1957** The Russians launch Sputnik.

IN BULGARIA	IN THE WORLD
	1966–69
	The Chinese Cultural Revolution
1971	
Zhivkov becomes president of Bulgaria.	
1984	
Zhivkov government forces Turkish	**1986**
minority to take Slavic names.	Nuclear power disaster at Chernobyl in Ukraine
1989	
Mass exodus of Bulgarian Turks. Foreign Minister Petar Mladenov ousts Zhivkov. Union of Democratic Forces (UDF) formed.	
1990	
Economic crisis. Communist Party becomes the Bulgarian Socialist Party (BSP). UDF's Zhelyu Zhelev becomes president.	
1991	**1991**
UDF wins election.	Breakup of the Soviet Union
1993	
Mass privatization program begins.	
1994	
BSP returns to power in general election.	
1997	**1997**
Mass protests over economic crisis. UDF leader Ivan Kostov becomes prime minister. Bulgarian currency pegged to German mark.	Hong Kong is returned to China.
2001	**2001**
Socialist Party leader Georgi Parvanov becomes president. Parliament agrees to destroy Soviet-made missiles by late 2002.	Terrorists crash planes in New York, Washington, D.C., and Pennsylvania.
2002	
Bulgaria formally invited to join NATO at the Prague summit.	**2003**
	War in Iraq begins.
2004	
Bulgaria is admitted to NATO.	
2005	
Bulgaria signs EU accession treaty and implements economic reforms.	
2007	
Bulgaria admitted to EU January 1.	

GLOSSARY

Bogomils (BOH-goh-mils)
Members of the medieval Bulgarian sect holding that God is the father of two sons—Jesus, the Savior, and Satan, the creator of the material world.

bolyar (or boyar) (BOH-lyahr)
A Bulgarian feudal lord.

Bulgars (BOOL-gahrs)
A nomadic tribe of Turanian origin, which formed a coalition with the Balkan Slavs and founded the Bulgarian state in A.D. 681.

chorbadjiya (chor-BAHD-ji-ya)
The richest Bulgarian in a village of the 19th century, often a collaborator of the local Turkish government.

Cyrillic (ser-IL-lik)
Based on the alphabet created by Saints Cyril and Methodius and used for the writing of the Slavic languages.

Day of Letters (also known as The Holiday of the Slavic Script and the Bulgarian press)
On May 24, an important national holiday when the Bulgarian nation celebrates education and learning and pays homage to Saints Cyril and Methodius.

glasnost (GLAHZ-nost)
Literally, "openness." The proclaimed public policy of openly and frankly discussing economic and political realities, first introduced in the former Soviet Union in 1985.

haidouk (hai-DOOK)
Member of the spontaneous underground movement against the Ottoman government, which started in the last decade of the 14th century.

horo (ho-RO)
A lively circular folk dance of many of the Balkan peoples.

Ignazhden
A festival on December 20 marking the first day of the Christmas holidays.

Nestinari (nays-ti-NAH-ri)
People with the gift of dancing on red-hot embers on May 21, Saints Constantine and Helena Day.

patriarch (PAY-tri-ark)
The head of the Bulgarian church.

perestroika (per-ah-STROY-kah)
Literally, "reformation." The transformation of the Communist economic and political system into a free-market democracy.

rakia (rah-KI-yah)
A Bulgarian grape or plum brandy popular as an aperitif.

survaki (SOOR-vah-ki)
A tradition observed on New Year's Day, when children visit their elders and family friends to wish them health and prosperity.

FURTHER INFORMATION

BOOKS

Daskalov, Roumen. *The Making of a Nation in the Balkans: Historiography of the Bulgarian Revival.* Budapest and New York: Central European University Press. 2004.

Dimitrov, Vesselin. *Bulgaria: The Uneven Transition.* London: Routledge, 2002.

Giatzidis, Emil. *An Introduction to Post-Communist Bulgaria: Political, Economic, and Social Transformations.* Manchester and New York: Manchester University Press, 2002.

Neuburger, Mary. *The Orient Within: Muslim Minorities and the Negotiation of Nationhood in Modern Bulgaria.* New York: Cornell University Press, 2004.

Rice, Timothy. *Music in Bulgaria: Experiencing Music, Expressing Culture.* New York: Oxford University Press, 2003.

WEB SITES

Bulgaria.com Home Page. www.bulgaria.com/

Bulgaria MSN Encarta. http://encarta.msn.com/encyclopedia_761556147/Bulgaria.html

Bulgarian National Parks. www.bulgariannationalparks.org/en/bnparks.phtml?context=category&ctg_id=25

Central Intelligence Agency World Factbook (select Bulgaria from country list). www.cia.gov/cia/publications/factbook/index.html

Discover Bulgaria. www.discover-bulgaria.com/

Library of Congress Country Studies. http://lcweb2.loc.gov/frd/cs/bgtoc.html

FILMS

A World In-between/ Mezhdinen svyat. Panaef, National Film Center, 1995.

Bay Ganyo Goes to Europe/ Bai Ganyo trugna po Evropa. Visual Creations, 1991.

Rio Adio. Boyana Film, 1989.

BIBLIOGRAPHY

Atlantic Monthly. "History's Cauldron." Atlantic Monthly 267:6 (June 1991), pp. 93–96.

Greenway, Paul. *Bulgaria*. Victoria, Australia: Lonely Planet Publications, 2004.

Kaplan, Robert. "Bulgaria: Tales from Communist Byzantium." Part 3 of *Balkan Ghosts: A Journey Through History*, pp. 193–230. New York: St. Martin's Press, 1993.

Resnick, Abraham. *Enchantment of the World: Bulgaria*. Chicago: Children's Press, 1995.

Tonchev, Belin (editor). *Young Poets of New Bulgaria: An Anthology*. Boston: Forest Books, 1990.

Walker, Brenda, with Belin Tonchev (trans.). *The Devil's Dozen: Thirteen Bulgarian Women Poets*. Boston: Forest Books, 1990.

United Nations. www.un.org

INDEX